Collins

Cambridge Lower Secondary

Maths

PROGRESS BOOK 7: TEACHER PACK

Author: Alastair Duncombe

William Collins' dream of knowledge for all began with the publication of his first book in 1819.
A self-educated mill worker, he not only enriched millions of lives, but also founded a flourishing publishing house.
Today, staying true to this spirit, Collins books are packed with inspiration, innovation and practical expertise.
They place you at the centre of a world of possibility and give you exactly what you need to explore it.

Collins. Freedom to teach.

Published by Collins

An imprint of HarperCollinsPublishers
The News Building, 1 London Bridge Street, London, SE1 9GF, UK

HarperCollinsPublishers
Macken House, 39/40 Mayor Street Upper, Dublin 1, D01 C9W8, Ireland

Browse the complete Collins catalogue at
collins.co.uk

© HarperCollins*Publishers* Limited 2024

10 9 8 7 6 5 4 3 2 1

ISBN 978-0-00-866713-9

British Library Cataloguing-in-Publication Data
A catalogue record for this publication is available from the British Library.

The questions, accompanying marks and mark schemes included in this resource have been written by the author and are for guidance only. They do not replicate examination papers and the questions in this resource will not appear in your exams. In examinations the way marks are awarded may be different. Any references to assessment and/or assessment preparation are the author's interpretation of the syllabus requirements.

This text has not been through the endorsement process for the Cambridge Pathway. Any references or materials related to answers, grades, papers or examinations are based on the opinion of the author. The Cambridge International Education syllabus or curriculum framework associated assessment guidance material and specimen papers should always be referred to for definitive guidance.

Author: Alastair Duncombe
Publisher: Elaine Higgleton
Product manager: Catherine Martin
Product developer: Saaleh Patel
Copyeditor: Eric Pradel
Proofreader: Tim Jackson
Cover designer: Gordon MacGilp
Cover illustrator: Ann Paganuzzi
Typesetter: Ken Vail Graphic Design
Production controller: Sarah Hovell
Printed and bound by Ashford Colour Press Ltd

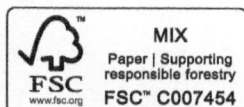

Content

Introduction

This *Stage 7 Progress Teacher Pack* (and the *Stage 7 Progress Student Book*) can be used to support the *Collins Cambridge Stage 7 Lower Secondary Maths course* or to supplement your own resources.

The *Progress Teacher Pack* contains

- six Assessment Tasks – each corresponding to 4 or 5 chapters in the Collins Cambridge Stage 7 Maths course
- two End of Book Tests: Paper 1 is a non-calculator paper and Paper 2 is a calculator-allowed paper
- student Self-assessment sheets for each of the Assessment Tasks and End of Book Tests
- mark schemes for each of the Assessment Tasks and for the End of Book Tests.

How to use the Progress resources

This photocopiable Teacher Pack contains a range of Assessment Tasks and Tests that are designed to be valuable and flexible formative and summative assessment resources. They can be used to identify strengths and weaknesses and to pinpoint how future teaching should be adjusted to ensure all students make good progress.

The six Assessment Tasks can be used as class tests or can be set for students to complete at home. Each Task includes a list of the topics being tested, and begins with some multiple-choice questions to build confidence and to check understanding of some of the key ideas. As the students work through each Task, the questions become increasingly challenging.

Some of the questions in each Task are written to address the Cambridge *Thinking and Working Mathematically* characteristics:
- Specialising and generalising
- Conjecturing and convincing
- Characterising and classifying
- Critiquing and improving.

These questions may involve more thought or may involve students justifying their answer by providing a clear explanation or working.

Each Task is designed to be marked out of 30 (if 4 chapters are covered) or 40 (if 5 chapters are covered). Teachers may wish to set a time limit of say 40 or 50 minutes for the Task if they are using it as a class test.

The End of Book tests assess objectives taught across the whole year. The style of the End of Book tests is otherwise the same as the Assessment Tasks, with a mixture of question styles and question difficulties, as well as the inclusion of some Thinking and Working Mathematically questions. These tests could be used for summative purposes as end of year examinations or as practice for students ahead of their examinations.

The *Progress Teacher Pack* includes clear mark schemes for each Task and for the End of Book Tests. These mark schemes contain notes on what should be seen for full marks to be awarded. They also set out how part marks can be awarded in a question where the full correct answer is not reached. In some questions, the mark schemes allow for 'follow through' marks to be awarded – these allow for students to score marks in the second part of a question if they have correctly made use of their wrong answer to the first part.

The student Self-assessment sheets give students the opportunity to reflect on their understanding. Students record the mark for each question in the grids and then use these to find how well they have done with the questions relating to each chapter (or, for the End of Book Tests, each mathematics strand). This allows students to then reflect on which parts of the test went well and which areas they found harder. Students could pick out particular chapters as strengths or weaknesses. They could also comment on their success with Thinking and Working Mathematically questions or how they did on calculator or non-calculator questions.

The Self-assessment sheets also prompt students to set two targets. Target setting can play an important role in formative assessment if the targets are considered carefully and are revisited periodically. Students may be tempted to state a quite general target. However, a more achievable (and therefore more useful) target would be something more specific. For example,

Less helpful targets…

To become more confident at decimals ✗

To avoid making needless errors ✗

More helpful targets…

To become more confident at dividing a decimal by a whole number ✓

To try to avoid making needless errors by underlining key words in the question ✓

Teachers can use the results of the test and the students' Self-assessment sheets to help them in future lesson planning. For example, if many students struggled with work linked to simplifying expressions, a teacher may wish to bear this in mind when planning their teaching of a related topic, such as solving equations – teachers could, for instance, include starter activities recapping the earlier work.

Key features: Assessment Tasks

Assessment Task 4

Answer **all** questions.
Total marks for this Assessment Task: 40

Topics tested:
Chapter 13: Calculations
Chapter 14: Functions and formulae
Chapter 15: Area and volume
Chapter 16: Fractions, decimals and percentages
Chapter 17: Probability 1

Part 1: Calculators not allowed

Do not use a calculator for this part of the Assessment Task.

1 Draw a ring around the value of 50 − (11 + 9).

    48   30   20

2 Here is a function machine.

    Input → × 4 → Output

Draw a ring around the output when the input is 8.

    2   12   32   84   [1]

3 Draw a ring around the value that cannot represent a probability.

    0        $\frac{1}{3}$ 45%   1.2   [1]

30

10 The diagram shows a shape made from joining a rectangle and a right-angled triangle.

Not to scale

2 cm
1 cm
4 cm
9 cm

The total area of the shape is x cm².

Show that x is a square number.

11 Add a set of brackets in this calculation to make it correct.

    7 + 4² + 5 × 2 = 49

33

Clear indication of which topics are being tested in each Assessment Task.

A mixture of questions where calculators are allowed and not allowed.

Each Task begins with some multiple-choice questions to boost confidence and to assess key ideas.

Each Task contains some questions that relate to Thinking and Working Mathematically (TWM).

Clear layout and simple language. Space for working out.

Key features: Student self-assessment sheets

Assessment Task 1: Self-assessment

Enter the mark for each question in the unshaded cells below.

Question	Negative numbers, indices and roots	2D and 3D shapes	Collecting data	Factors and rational numbers
1				
2				
3				
4				
5				
6				
7				
8				
9				
10				
11				
12				
13				
14				
15				
16				
17				
18				
19				
20				
Total	/10	/9	/4	/7

Some of the questions test your skills at Thinking and Working Mathematically. Write your marks for these questions in the grid below.

Question number	6	7	8	14	16(b)	17	18	20	Total
Thinking and working mathematically									/13

> Clear table to link the marks scored on each question to the relevant textbook chapter/topic.

> By totalling each column, students can compare how well they have scored in each topic area.

> Success in the Thinking and Working Mathematically questions can also be analysed.

The areas of the test that I am pleased with are

The areas of the test that I found harder are

Set yourself TWO targets.

TARGET 1

TARGET 2

> Space for students to reflect on how they have done and set targets.

Key features: Mark schemes

> Clear indication of the correct answer and number of marks to be awarded.

> Guidance given about awarding follow through marks.

> Guidance given about how to award part marks.

> Further information given where required about what is expected for full marks.

Question	Answer	Mark	Part marks
	65 cm²	2	Award 1 mark for sight of area of a relevant triangle or rectangle: 33 or 24 or 8 or 12 or 9
26(a)	0.55	2	Award 1 mark for $\frac{44}{80}$ or equivalent fraction or $44 \div 80$ or answer of 0.45
	frequency > 80 and heads : tails = 11 : 9 For example, • 88 heads and 72 tails • 55 heads and 45 tails.	1FT	Follow through their part (a) – accept tables that give the same relative frequency as found in (a) provided total frequency > 80
27	3500 (South African rand)		Award 1 mark for $\frac{27195}{3100}$ or 8.75 or $\frac{3106}{17125}$ or equivalent or for $\frac{400}{3100}$ or $\frac{3100}{400}$ or equivalent.
28	An accurate drawing of the trapezium.		Tolerance of 2 mm on lengths and 2° on angles. Award 1 mark for at least one accurately drawn length (8.5 cm or 4.2 cm) and at least one accurately drawn angle (52° or 74°).
29	7(9h)	2	Award 1 mark for sight of 21
30	$a = 2, b = -1$ and $c = 7$ and $a + b + c = 8$ (which is a multiple of 4)	3	Award 2 marks for sight of 2 of $a = 2, b = -1$ and $c = 7$ or Award 1 mark for sight of $a = 2$ or $b = -1$ or $c = 7$ or Award 1 mark for 8 right, 5 down.

Assessment Task 1

Answer **all** questions.
Total marks for this Assessment Task: 30
You will need mathematical instruments.

Do **not** use a calculator for this Assessment Task.

> Topics tested:
> Chapter 1: Factors
> Chapter 2: 2D and 3D shapes
> Chapter 3: Collecting data
> Chapter 4: Negative numbers and indices

1   Draw a ring around the number that is a multiple of 9

           102   142   168   261

[1]

2   The diagram shows a circle with centre O.

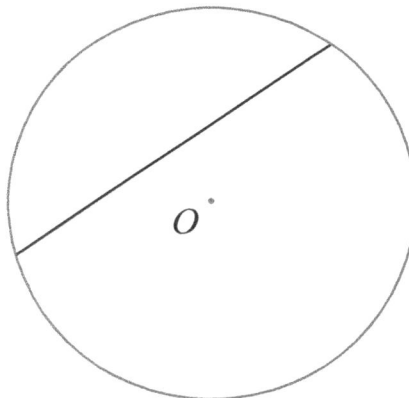

Draw a ring around the name given to the line that has been drawn inside the circle.

    circumference   chord   diameter   radius

[1]

3   Draw a ring around the value of $\sqrt{64}$

           4   8   16   32

[1]

4 Mario wants to find out what nurses working in his hospital think about how much they are paid.

He selects 30 nurses from his hospital at random.

Draw a ring around the population in Mario's study.

All nurses that work in his hospital   All people that work in his hospital

The 30 nurses he selects   All nurses in the country

[1]

5 A 3D shape has 1 curved surface and 2 circular faces.

Draw a ring around a type of shape that it could be.

sphere   pyramid   cylinder   cone

[1]

6 Draw a ring around an example of continuous data.

the colour of a bus   the number of passengers on the bus

the length of a bus   the type of fuel used by the bus

[1]

7 Work out:

$8 \div (-2)$

_____

[1]

8 Complete the following working to find the lowest common multiple of 12 and 15.

First 6 multiples of 12 are: 12, 24, _____, _____, _____, _____

First 6 multiples of 15 are: 15, 30, _____, _____, _____, _____

The lowest common multiple of 12 and 15 is _____

[2]

9   Sanjay is investigating what members of his gym think about the equipment.

(a)   He decides to collect data using one of these two methods.

Method 1	**Method 2**
Ask every member of his gym what they think.	Ask a sample of gym members what they think.

Give a reason why he may prefer to use Method 2.

_____

_____

[1]

(b)   The gym has 500 members.
Sanjay suggests collecting data from 10 members.

Tick (✓) a box below to show if Sanjay's sample size is appropriate or not.

Appropriate sample size ☐   Not an appropriate sample size ☐

Give a reason for your answer.

_____

_____

[1]

10 The diagram shows two congruent triangles.

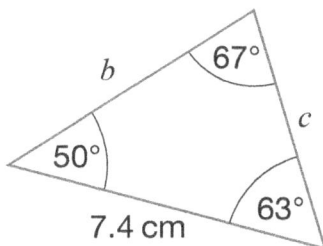

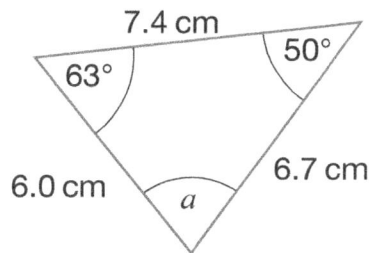

7.4 cm

b 67°

c

50°

63°

7.4 cm

63°   50°

6.0 cm a 6.7 cm

Not to scale

Tick (✓) to show if each statement is true or false.

	True	**False**
Angle $a = 67°$	☐	☐
Side length $b = 6.0$ cm	☐	☐
Side length $c = 6.7$ cm	☐	☐

[1]

11 Here is a list of integers.

$$2 \quad -2 \quad -3 \quad 4 \quad -4 \quad -7 \quad 8 \quad 14$$

Use four of these integers to complete these calculations.
Use each integer no more than once.

_____ × _____ = −28

_____ × _____ = −28

[1]

12 Here is a circle and a radius OA.

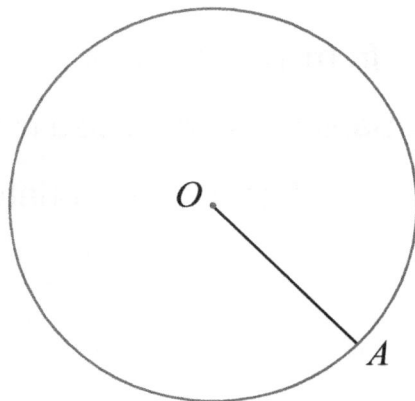

Not to scale

(a) Line L passes through A and is perpendicular to OA.

Draw line L on the circle.

[1]

(b) Write down the mathematical name for line L.

_____

[1]

13 Draw lines to match each calculation with its answer.

$-12 - 26$ -38

$-12 - (-26)$ -14

$26 - (-12)$ 14

$-7 - 7$ 38

[1]

14 Here are three prisms.

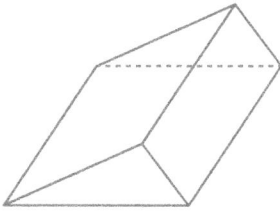 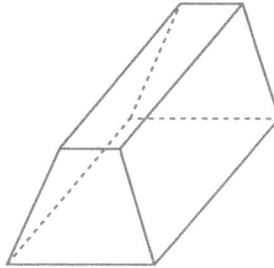 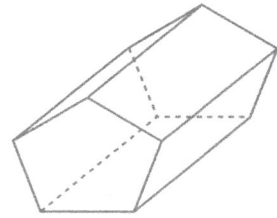

_____ edges   _____ edges   _____ edges

Find the number of edges for each prism and then complete the statement.

The number of edges of a prism must always be a multiple of _____

[2]

15 Find the value of $\sqrt[3]{125} - 5^2$

_____

[2]

16 Find a number between 5010 and 5020 that is a multiple of 8

_____

[1]

17 Samira designs a questionnaire to find out information about how frequently people go to the supermarket.

Here is one of her questions and the tick boxes.

Question → | How many times do you go to the supermarket?
Tick (✓) a box.
Tick boxes → 1 to 2 ☐   3 to 4 ☐   4 or more ☐

(a) Explain how Samira could improve her question.

_____

_____

[1]

(b) Explain what is wrong with Samira's tick boxes.

_____

_____

[1]

18 ■ represents a square number.

◆ represents a cube number.

■ + ◆ = 63

Find the value of ■ − ◆

_____

[2]

19 Ellie has 48 yellow counters and 72 red counters.

She wants to divide these counters into pots such that:

- she uses all her counters
- each pot contains exactly the same number of yellow counters
- each pot contains exactly the same number of red counters.

(a) Find the largest number of pots Ellie can use.

_____

[2]

(b) Find the total number of counters that would be in each pot.

_____

[1]

20 Here is a rule for testing if a number is divisible by 7.

> Remove the last digit from the number and double it.
>
> Subtract this from the remaining number.
>
> If the answer is divisible by 7, then so was the original number.

Use this rule to show that 672 is divisible by 7.

[2]

Total marks: $\frac{}{30}$

Assessment Task 1: Self-assessment

Enter the mark for each question in the unshaded cells below.

Question	Factors	2D and 3D shapes	Collecting data	Negative numbers and indices
1				
2				
3				
4				
5				
6				
7				
8				
9				
10				
11				
12				
13				
14				
15				
16				
17				
18				
19				
20				
Total	/9	/7	/6	/8

Some of the questions test your skills at Thinking and Working Mathematically. Write your marks for these questions in the grid below.

Question number	9(a)	9(b)	13	14	16	17(a)	17(b)	20	Total
Thinking and working mathematically									/10

The areas of the test that I am pleased with are

_____

_____

_____

The areas of the test that I found harder are

_____

_____

_____

Set yourself TWO targets.

TARGET 1

_____

_____

TARGET 2

_____

_____

Assessment Task 2

Answer **all** questions.
Total marks for this Assessment Task: 30
You will need mathematical instruments.
You may find tracing paper helpful.

Do **not** use a calculator for this Assessment Task.

> Topics tested:
> Chapter 5: Expressions
> Chapter 6: Symmetry
> Chapter 7: Rounding and decimals
> Chapter 8: Presenting and interpreting data 1

1 Here is an expression: $2x + y + 3$

Draw a ring around the number of terms in this expression.

      1   2   3   4

[1]

2 Draw a ring around the number of lines of symmetry in a regular octagon.

      1   2   4   8

[1]

3 Draw a ring around the value that is the same as 2×10^2

      20   40   200   400

[1]

4 A bag contains b books.
Anushka removes 2 books from the bag.

Draw a ring around the expression for the number of books now in the bag.

      $b + 2$ $b - 2$ $2b$ $\dfrac{b}{2}$

[1]

5 Draw a ring around the value of −0.4 + 0.9

0.5   −0.5   −1.3   1.3

[1]

6 Lauren sells jumpers.

The Venn diagram shows some information about the number of red jumpers and the number of large jumpers she sold last week.

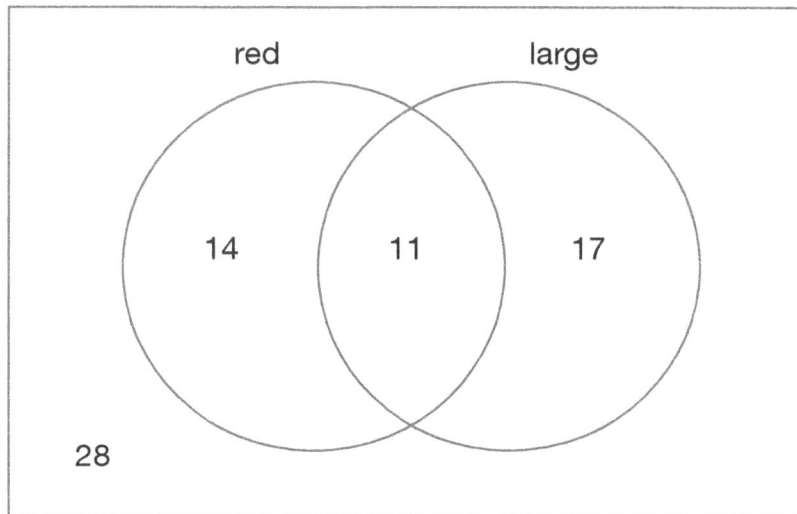

Draw a ring around the number of red jumpers Lauren sold last week.

11   14   25   28

[1]

7 Here are four decimals.

0.516   0.5137   0.5145   0.51542

Write each decimal in the correct position in the table.

Rounds to 0.51 (to 2 decimal places)	Rounds to 0.52 (to 2 decimal places)

[2]

8 Find the value of $3c$, when $c = 6$

_____

[1]

9 Calculate 0.4×116

_____

[2]

10 The two-way table shows some information about the favourite subjects for students in Class A and students in Class B.

	Science	Maths	Art	History	Other
Class A	7	4	6	5	
Class B	6	8	8	2	5

(a) There are 30 students in Class A.

Complete the table.

[1]

(b) Find the total number of students in the two classes that gave Science or Maths as their favourite subject.

_____

[1]

11 Find the value of $318 \div 10^4$

_____

[1]

12 Here are the values of a and b.

$a = 6$ $b = 2$

Complete each statement by writing an expression involving **both** a and b.
One has been done for you.

$2a + b$ .... $= 14$

.... $= 10$

.... $= 3$

[2]

13 (a) Here are two shapes.

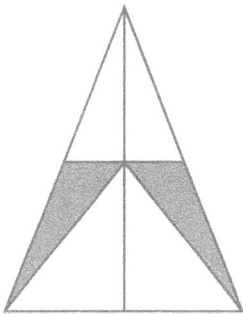   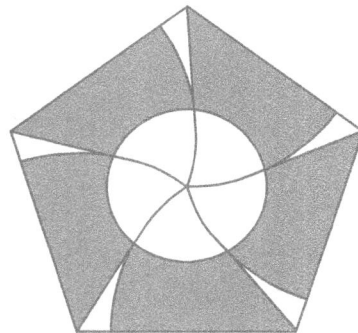

Order _____   Order _____

Write down the order of rotational symmetry for each shape.

[2]

(b) Here is a square divided into 16 smaller squares, with two of them shaded.

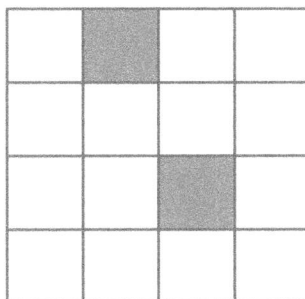

Shade exactly **six** more small squares to give a design with rotational
symmetry of order 2 and no lines of symmetry.

[2]

14 Pari, Mel and Kieron each think of a number.

Pari's number is a.
Mel's number is b.
Kieron's number is c.

They each do some calculations on their number.

Complete the table by writing in the missing expressions and numbers.
The first one has been done for you.

	Expression
Pari multiplies her number by 2	$2a$
Mel multiplies her number by 5 and then subtracts 2	
Kieron multiplies his number by _____ and then adds _____	$4c + 9$

[2]

15 Maxine grows two types of potato plant in her garden.

The table shows how many small potatoes and how many large potatoes her plants produced this year.

	Small	Large
Type A	15	9
Type B	23	11

Draw a compound bar chart to represent this information.
Remember to complete the key.

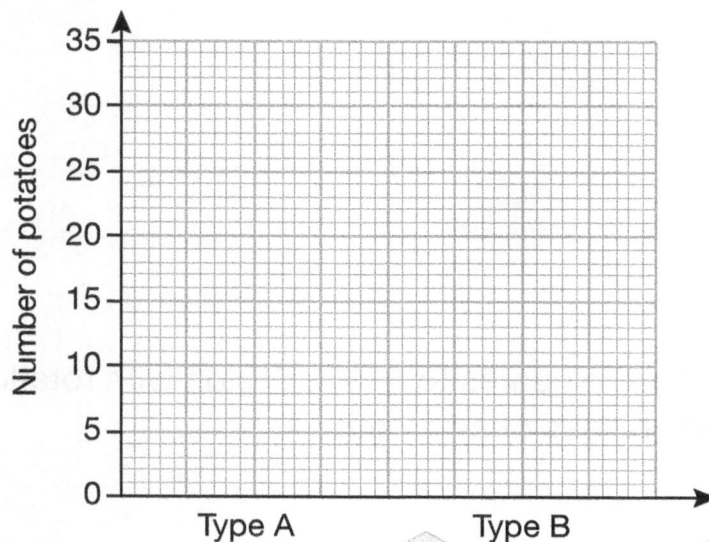

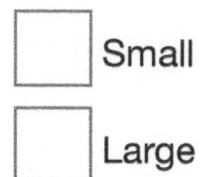

Key:

☐ Small

☐ Large

[2]

16 Calculate $21.34 \div 9$

Give your answer to 3 decimal places.

_____

[2]

17 The values of x, y and z are:

$x = 8$, $y = 6$ and $z = 5$

Find the value of $xy - 3z$

_____

[2]

18 The frequency diagram shows the hand span (in centimetres) of a group of students.

Show that over half of the students have a hand span of less than 18.5 cm.

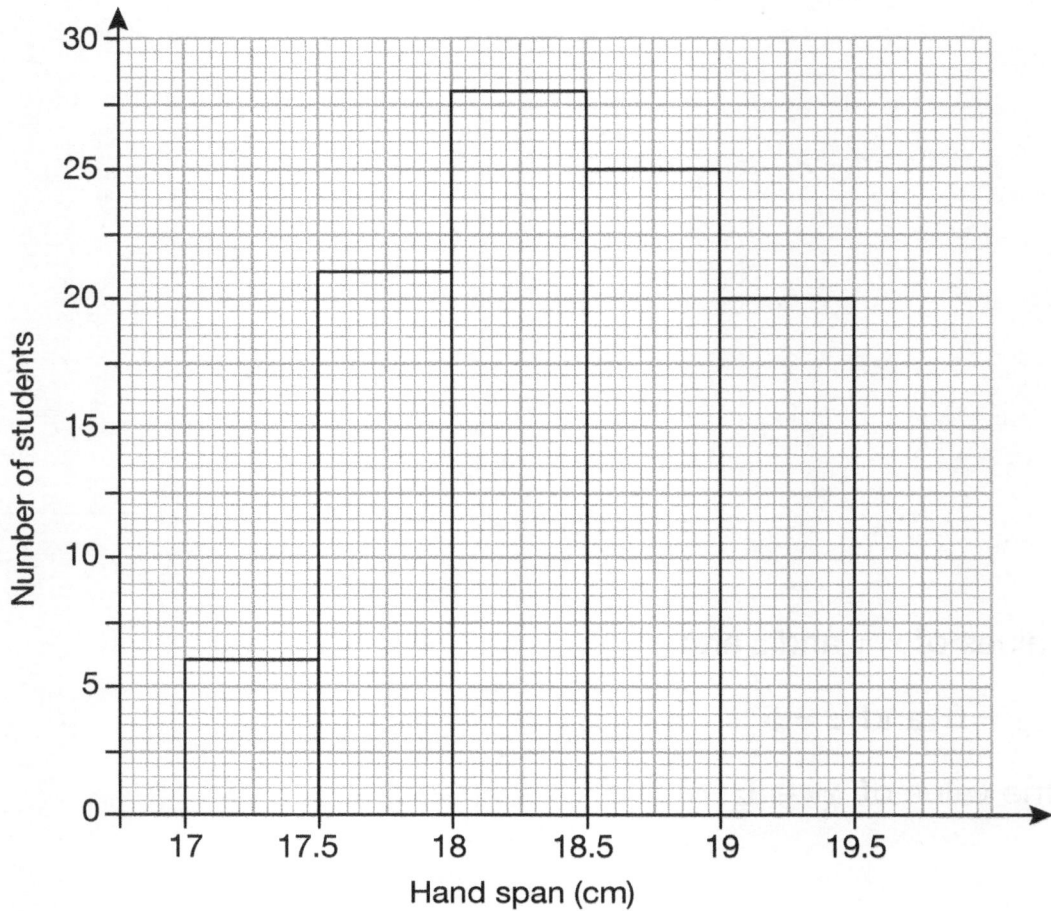

[2]

Total marks: ——— / 30

Assessment Task 2: Self-assessment

Enter the mark for each question in the unshaded cells below.

Question	Expressions	Symmetry	Rounding and decimals	Presenting and interpreting data 1
1				
2				
3				
4				
5				
6				
7				
8				
9				
10				
11				
12				
13				
14				
15				
16				
17				
18				
Total	/9	/5	/9	/7

Some of the questions test your skills at Thinking and Working Mathematically. Write your marks for these questions in the grid below.

Question number	7	12	13(b)	18	Total
Thinking and working mathematically					/8

The areas of the test that I am pleased with are

_____

_____

_____

The areas of the test that I found harder are

_____

_____

_____

Set yourself TWO targets.

TARGET 1

_____

_____

TARGET 2

_____

_____

Assessment Task 3

Answer **all** questions.
Total marks for this Assessment Task: 30

> Topics tested:
> Chapter 9: Fractions
> Chapter 10: Manipulating expressions
> Chapter 11: Angles
> Chapter 12: Measures of average and spread

Part 1: Calculators not allowed

Do not use a calculator for this part of the Assessment Task.

1 Draw a ring around the answer to $1\frac{2}{7} + 1\frac{3}{7}$

$2\frac{5}{7}$ $1\frac{5}{7}$ $2\frac{5}{14}$ $1\frac{5}{14}$

[1]

2 Draw a ring around the size of angle a.

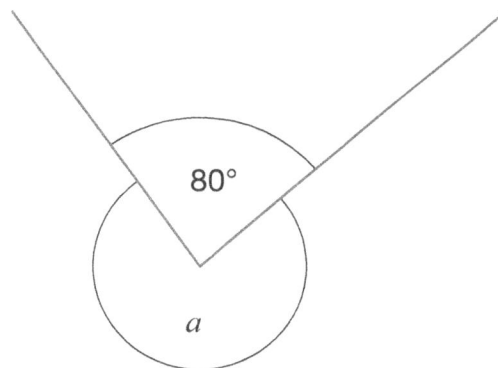

Not to scale

$100°$ $120°$ $220°$ $280°$

[1]

3 Draw a ring around the fraction that is the value of $\frac{2}{7} \times \frac{1}{3}$

$\frac{3}{21}$ $\frac{2}{21}$ $\frac{3}{10}$ $\frac{2}{10}$

[1]

4 The table shows the marks that a group of students obtained in a test.

Marks	Number of students
5	11
6	8
7	6
8	3
9	2

(a) Write down the modal mark.

_____

[1]

(b) Find the range of the marks.

_____

[1]

5 Tick (✓) to show if the answer to each calculation is less than 1 or greater than 1.

	Less than 1	Greater than 1
$1\frac{1}{10} + \frac{1}{5}$	☐	☐
$\frac{1}{3} \times \frac{1}{2}$	☐	☐
$\frac{1}{2} \div \frac{1}{4}$	☐	☐

[1]

6 Simplify.

$m \times m \times m =$ _____

[1]

7 Calculate.

$$\frac{2}{3} \div \frac{5}{12}$$

Give your answer in its simplest form.

_____

8 The diagram shows a parallelogram.

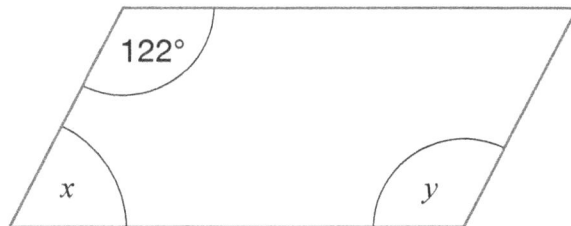

Not to scale

Calculate the size of angles x and y.

$x = $ _____ $^\circ$

$y = $ _____ $^\circ$

[2]

9 A bucket contains $2\frac{5}{6}$ litres of water.

Mia adds $1\frac{7}{10}$ litres of water to the bucket.

Show that the bucket now contains $4\frac{8}{15}$ litres of water.

[2]

10 Simplify.

$$\frac{n}{3} + \frac{4n}{9}$$

[2]

Part 2: Calculators allowed

You may use a calculator for this part of the Assessment Task.

11 Simplify $6h \times 2$

Draw a ring around your answer.

$8h$	$12h$	$6h^2$	$36h^2$

[1]

12 The diagram shows two parallel lines, an angle marked t and four shaded angles.

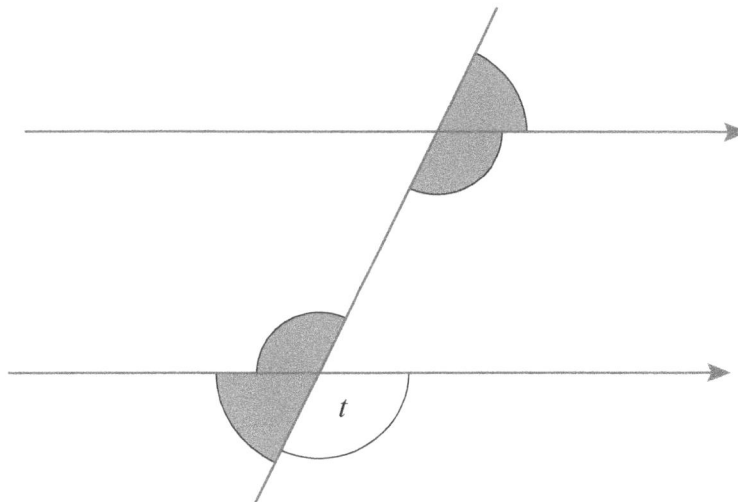

How many of the shaded angles are equal in size to angle t?

Draw a ring around your answer.

1	2	3	4

[1]

13 Draw a ring around the expression equivalent to $2(k + 3)$

$k^2 + 6$	$k^2 + 5$	$2k + 5$	$2k + 6$

[1]

14 Dev records the number of glasses of water 15 people drink one day.

3	1	2	2	5	0	1	0
4	6	0	1	2	4	3	

Find the median number of glasses of water.

_____

[2]

15 The lines ABC and BD are perpendicular.

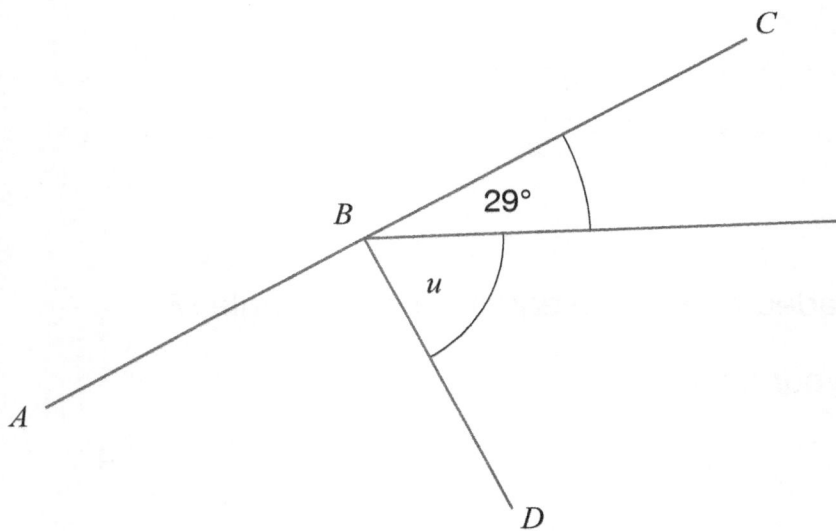

Not to scale

29°

Find the size of angle u.

$u =$ _____°

[1]

16 The table shows the number of trees in each of 50 gardens.

Number of trees	Number of gardens
0	9
1	18
2	12
3	6
4	5

(a) Calculate the mean number of trees in a garden.

_____

[2]

(b) Another garden has 10 trees.

Tina calculates the mean, median, mode and range for the number of trees in the 51 gardens.

She compares these values with the values for the original 50 gardens.

Some of the values are different and some of the values are the same.

Tick (✓) to show which values are different and which are the same.

	Different	The same
Mean	☐	☐
Median	☐	☐
Mode	☐	☐
Range	☐	☐

[2]

17 The diagram shows two parallel lines and a transversal.

Not to scale

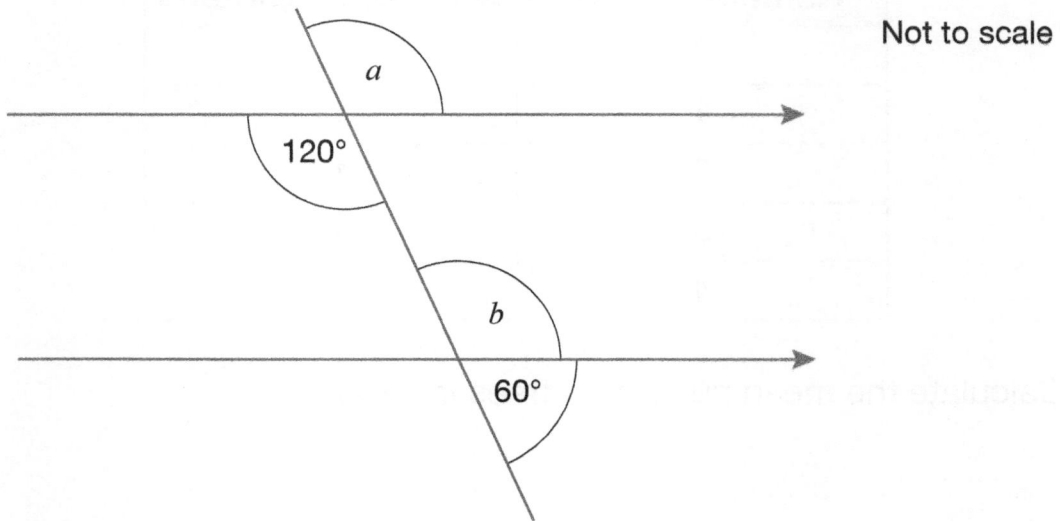

Write down the size of angles a and b.

$a =$ _____ °

$b =$ _____ °

[1]

18 Simplify each expression.

$4(3x - 2) + 8$

_____

$11 - 5a - 2 + 3a$

_____

[2]

19 Calculate the size of angle x.

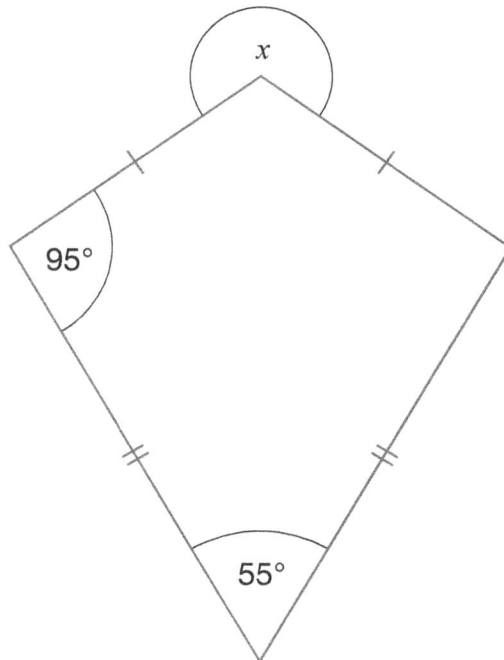

Not to scale

$x =$ _____°

[2]

Total marks: $\dfrac{}{30}$

27

Assessment Task 3: Self-assessment

Enter the marks for each question in the unshaded cells below.

Question	Fractions	Manipulating expressions	Angles	Measures of average and spread
1				
2				
3				
4				
5				
6				
7				
8				
9				
10				
11				
12				
13				
14				
15				
16				
17				
18				
19				
Total	/7	/7	/8	/8

Some of the questions test your skills at Thinking and Working Mathematically.
Write your marks for these questions in the grid below.

Question number	5	9	12	16(b)	Total
Thinking and working mathematically					/6

The areas of the test that I am pleased with are

_____

_____

_____

The areas of the test that I found harder are

_____

_____

_____

Set yourself TWO targets.

TARGET 1

_____

_____

TARGET 2

_____

_____

Assessment Task 4

Answer **all** questions.
Total marks for this Assessment Task: 40

Topics tested:
Chapter 13: Calculations
Chapter 14: Functions and formulae
Chapter 15: Area and volume
Chapter 16: Fractions, decimals and percentages
Chapter 17: Probability 1

Part 1: Calculators not allowed

Do not use a calculator for this part of the Assessment Task.

1 Draw a ring around the value of 50 − (11 + 9)

   48   30   20   −30

   [1]

2 Here is a function machine.

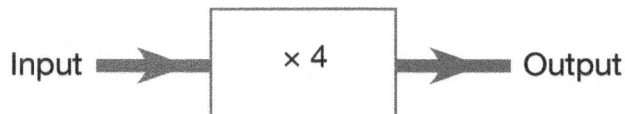

   Input ➡ | × 4 | ➡ Output

   Draw a ring around the output when the input is 8

   2   12   32   84

   [1]

3 Draw a ring around the value that cannot represent a probability.

   0                $\frac{1}{3}$ 45%   1.2

   [1]

4 Complete the table to show equivalent fractions, decimals and percentages.

Fraction	Decimal	Percentage
	0.75	
$\frac{3}{10}$		
		9%

[2]

5 Calculate.

(a) 0.35 + 0.8 + 0.65 + 2.2

_____

[1]

(b) $\frac{2}{3}$ × 11 × 3

_____

[1]

6 Write a number on the answer line to make a correct statement.

1 hectare < _____ m² < 2 hectares

[1]

7 Write a number in each gap to make correct statements.

$(7^2 + 2 × 3) ÷ 5 =$ _____

(11 − _____) × (9 + 3) = 36

[2]

8 **(a)** Show that $\frac{5}{6} > \frac{37}{48}$

[1]

(b) Here are four fractions.

$\frac{19}{48}$ $\qquad$ $\frac{1}{3}$ $\qquad$ $\frac{11}{24}$ $\qquad$ $\frac{5}{12}$

Complete each sentence by writing one of the four fractions.

The smallest fraction is _____

The largest fraction is _____

[1]

9 There are 5 vowels (A, E, I, O and U) in the English language alphabet.

Tariq has 10 cards.

A	K	T	P	W
C	F	U	J	H

Liz gives Tariq two more cards with a letter on each.

The letters on these cards are not shown.

Tariq says, "If I now pick up one of my 12 cards at random, the probability it is a vowel is 0.25"

Write a letter on the two cards above to make Tariq's statement true.

[1]

10 The diagram shows a shape made from joining a rectangle and a right-angled triangle.

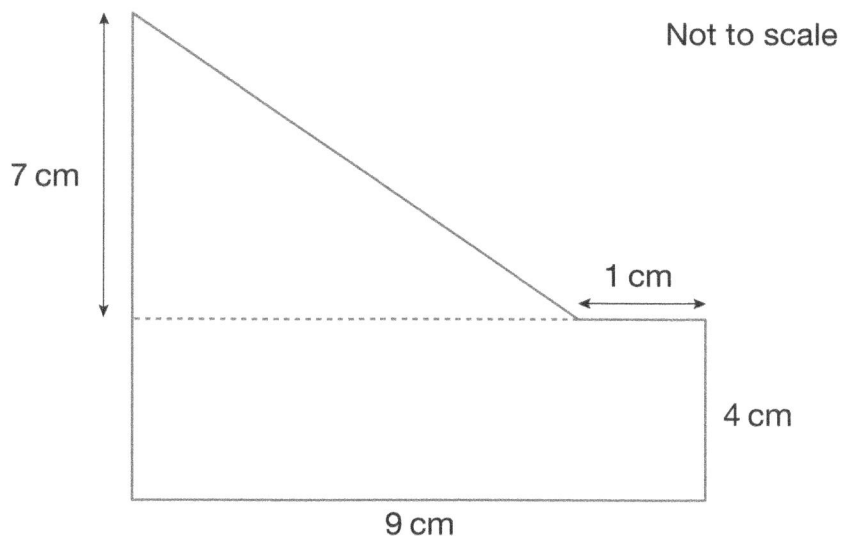

Not to scale

7 cm

1 cm

4 cm

9 cm

The total area of the shape is x cm².

Show that x is a square number.

[3]

11 Add a set of brackets in this calculation to make it correct.

$$7 + 4^2 + 5 \times 2 = 49$$

[1]

12 Here is a decimal number:

1.035

(a) Write 1.035 as a percentage.

_____%

[1]

(b) Write 1.035 as an improper fraction.

Give your answer in its simplest form.

_____

[2]

Part 2: Calculators allowed

You may use a calculator for this part of the Assessment Task.

13 An ordinary, fair six-sided dice is thrown.

Draw a ring around the probability of throwing a 4.

$\dfrac{1}{6}$ $\qquad\qquad$ $\dfrac{1}{4}$ $\qquad\qquad$ $\dfrac{4}{6}$ $\qquad\qquad$ $\dfrac{1}{2}$

[1]

14 The diagram shows a triangle.

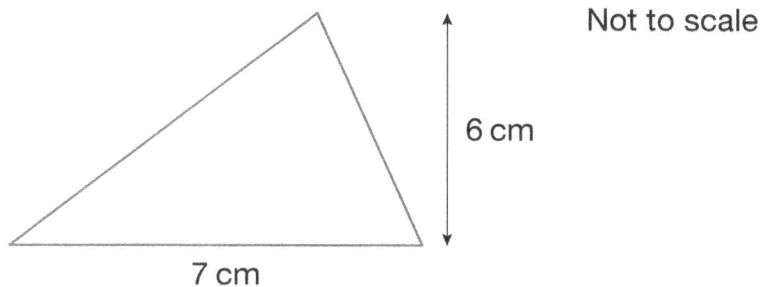

Not to scale

6 cm

7 cm

Draw a ring around the area of the triangle.

10.5 cm² $\qquad$ 13 cm² $\qquad$ 21 cm² $\qquad$ 42 cm²

[1]

15 Draw a ring around the formula for the number, h, of hours in d days.

$h = \dfrac{d}{24}$ $\qquad$ $h = 24d$ $\qquad$ $h = 2 + 24$ $\qquad$ $h = d - 24$

[1]

16 Insert one of the symbols

$=$ **or** $\neq$

to compare each fraction and decimal.

The first one has been done for you.

$\dfrac{1}{6}$ _____ $\neq$ _____ 0.2

$\dfrac{11}{20}$ _____ 0.55

$\dfrac{7}{8}$ _____ 0.875

$\dfrac{5}{16}$ _____ 0.315

[2]

17 Here are three words:

COOKBOOK   REAPPEAR   WELLNESS

A letter is picked at random from each word.

Complete the table by listing the possible outcomes for each word and tick (✓) to show if the outcomes are equally likely or not.

The first row is completed for you.

Word	List of possible outcomes	Outcomes equally likely	Outcomes not equally likely
COOKBOOK	C, O, K, B	☐	✓
REAPPEAR	_____	☐	☐
WELLNESS	_____	☐	☐

[2]

18 A bag contains 8 balls.

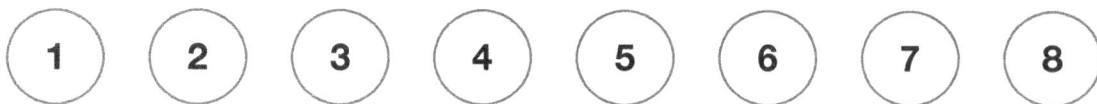

$\begin{pmatrix} 1 \end{pmatrix}$ $\begin{pmatrix} 2 \end{pmatrix}$ $\begin{pmatrix} 3 \end{pmatrix}$ $\begin{pmatrix} 4 \end{pmatrix}$ $\begin{pmatrix} 5 \end{pmatrix}$ $\begin{pmatrix} 6 \end{pmatrix}$ $\begin{pmatrix} 7 \end{pmatrix}$ $\begin{pmatrix} 8 \end{pmatrix}$

Without looking in the bag, Martina picks a ball at random.

Tick (✓) to show if each of these statements is true or false.

Statement	True	False
It is probable that Martina will pick a number greater than 2.	☐	☐
It is possible that Martina will pick a number that is a factor of 9.	☐	☐
It is equally likely that Martina will pick a square number as it is that she picks an odd number.	☐	☐

[1]

19 **(a)** Here is an inequality for a decimal number x.

$$1.49 < x < 1.5$$

Write down a possible value for x.

_____

[1]

(b) Here is an inequality for a mixed number y.

$$2\frac{1}{10} < y < 2\frac{1}{5}$$

Write down a possible value for y.

_____

[1]

20 Write these areas in order of size, starting with the **smallest**.

$0.04\,\text{m}^2$ $\qquad\qquad$ $5\,\text{cm}^2$ $\qquad\qquad$ $700\,\text{mm}^2$

_____ $\qquad$ _____ $\qquad$ _____

smallest $\qquad$ → $\qquad\qquad\qquad$ → $\qquad$ largest

[1]

21 The diagram shows a cuboid.

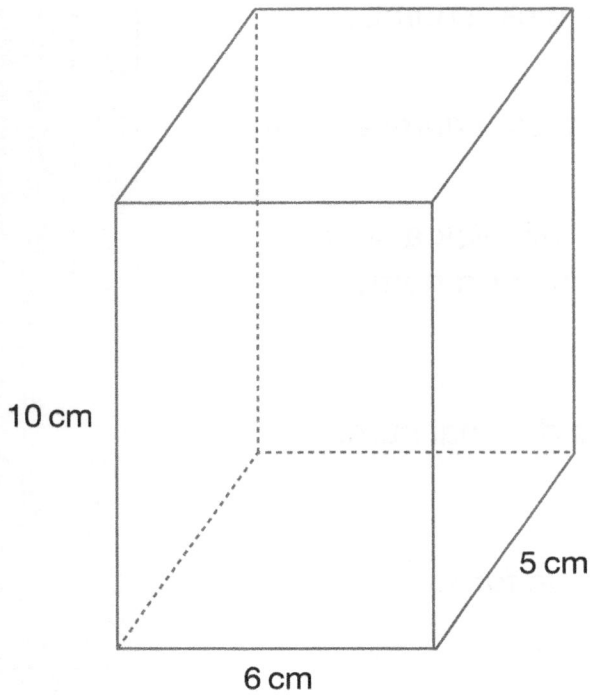

Not to scale

10 cm

5 cm

6 cm

Calculate the total surface area of the cuboid.

_____ cm²

[3]

22 Here are two function machines.

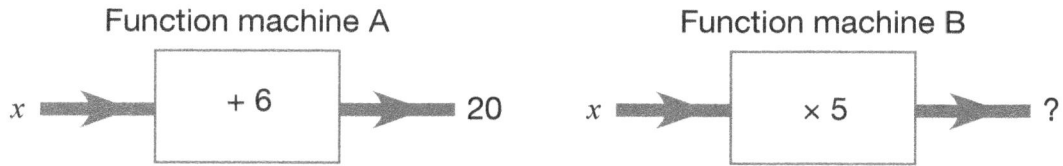

Function machine A

$x \rightarrow \boxed{+6} \rightarrow 20$

Function machine B

$x \rightarrow \boxed{\times 5} \rightarrow ?$

When x is the input to function machine A, the output is 20.

Find the output when the same value of x is the input to function machine B.

_____

[2]

23 Biscuits are packed into packets.

The number of biscuits, b, in p packets is given by the formula $b = 6p$

The packets of biscuits are packed into boxes.
10 packets of biscuits are packed into each box.

Find a formula for the number of biscuits, b, in n boxes.

$b =$ _____

[1]

24 Here are two cuboids.

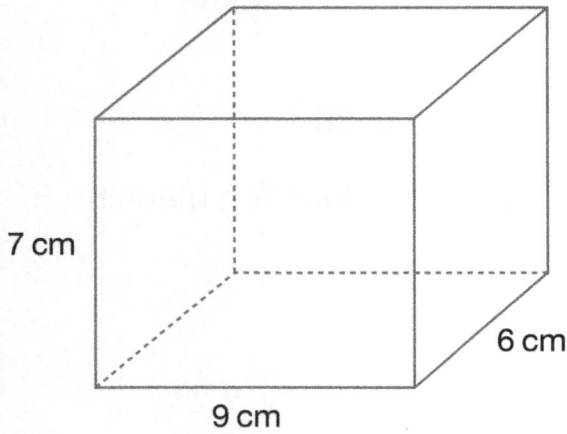

7 cm

6 cm

9 cm

Cuboid A

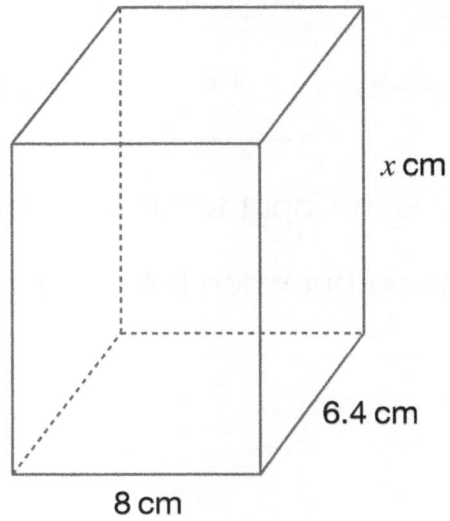

Not to scale

x cm

6.4 cm

8 cm

Cuboid B

volume of cuboid B = volume of cuboid A + 6 cm³

Find the value of x.

$x =$ _____

[3]

Total marks: ——
                40

Assessment Task 4: Self-assessment

Enter the marks for each question in the unshaded cells below.

Question	Calculations	Functions and formulae	Area and volume	Fractions, decimals and percentages	Probability 1
1					
2					
3					
4					
5					
6					
7					
8					
9					
10					
11					
12					
13					
14					
15					
16					
17					
18					
19					
20					
21					
22					
23					
24					
Total	/6	/5	/12	/11	/6

Some of the questions test your skills at Thinking and Working Mathematically. Write your marks for these questions in the grid below.

Question number	6	8(a)	9	10	18	19(a)	19(b)	Total
Thinking and working mathematically								/9

The areas of the test that I am pleased with are

_____

_____

_____

The areas of the test that I found harder are

_____

_____

_____

Set yourself TWO targets.

TARGET 1

_____

_____

TARGET 2

_____

_____

Assessment Task 5

Answer **all** questions.
Total marks for this Assessment Task: 40
You will need mathematical instruments.
Tracing paper may be used.

Topics tested:
Chapter 18: Transformations
Chapter 19: Percentages
Chapter 20: Presenting and interpreting data 2
Chapter 21: Equations and inequalities
Chapter 22: Ratio and proportion

Part 1: Calculators not allowed

Do not use a calculator for this part of the Assessment Task.

1   The point A has coordinates (5, 9).

Point A is translated 2 units right and 3 units down.

Draw a ring around the coordinates of the image of A.

    (7, 12)   (7, 6)   (3, 12)   (3, 6)

[1]

2   Here is an equation.

$$3x = 12$$

Draw a ring around the value of x.

    $x = 3$ $x = 4$ $x = 9$ $x = 36$

[1]

3   A bus ticket increases by 25%

What is the new cost of the ticket as a percentage of the original cost?
Draw a ring around your answer.

    1.25%   25%   75%   125%

[1]

4 A school football team plays five matches.

The line graph shows the number of parents watching each match.

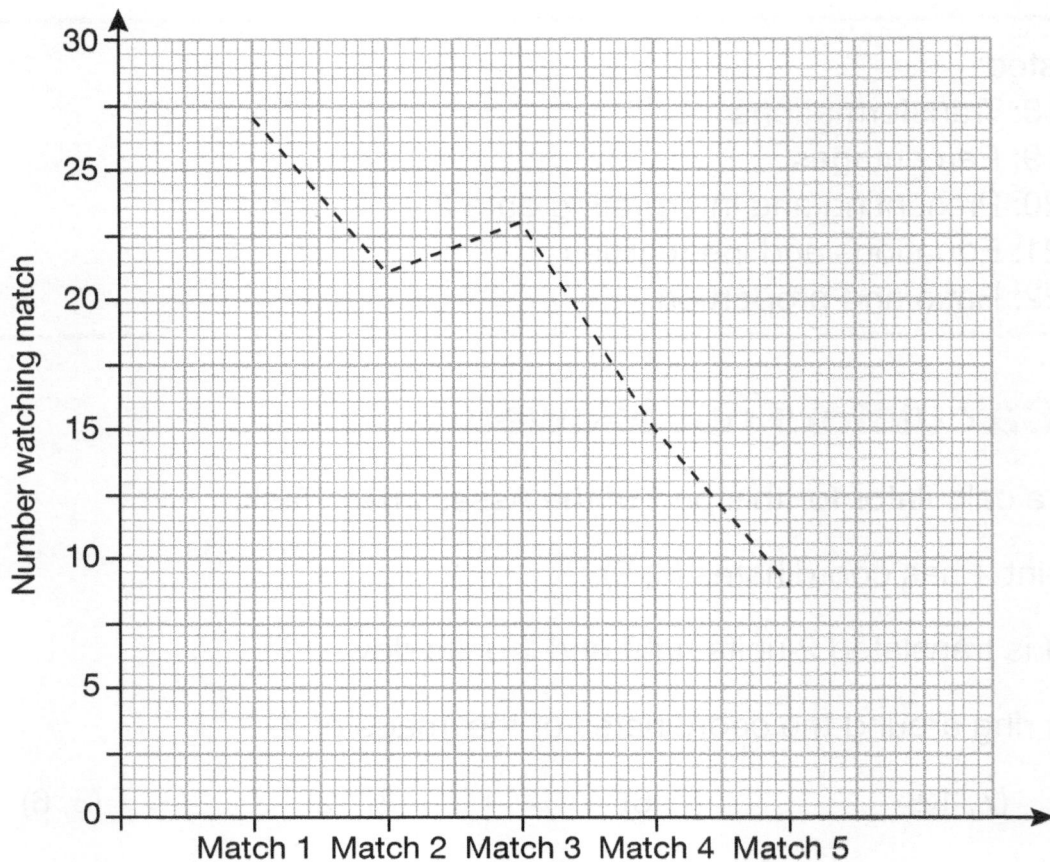

Find how many more parents watched Match 1 than watched Match 5.

_____

[2]

5 Find 0.5% of 800

_____

[1]

6 Here are five statements about ratios.

Draw lines to show whether each statement is true or false.
The first one has been done for you.

Statement A
$12 : 15 = 4 : 5$

Statement B
$18 : 24 = 3 : 4$

Statement C
$4 : 6 = 3 : 5$

Statement D
$1.5 : 3 = 1 : 2$

Statement E
$0.6 : 0.4 = 2 : 3$

True

False

[2]

7 **(a)** Show the inequality $x < 7$ on the number line.

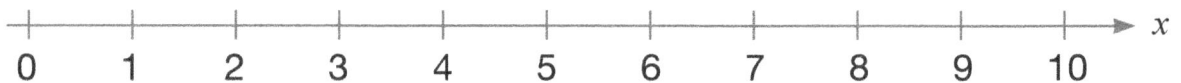

[1]

(b) Write an inequality to describe the interval shown on the number line.

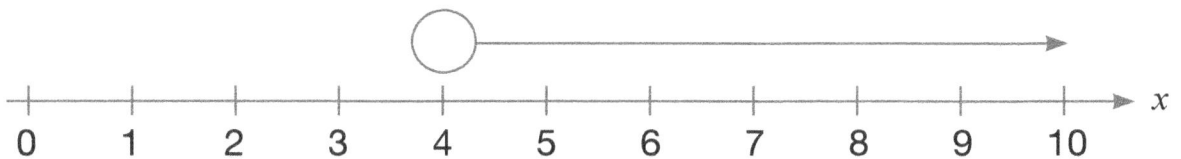

_____

[1]

8 **(a)** Rotate triangle T about the centre O by 180°

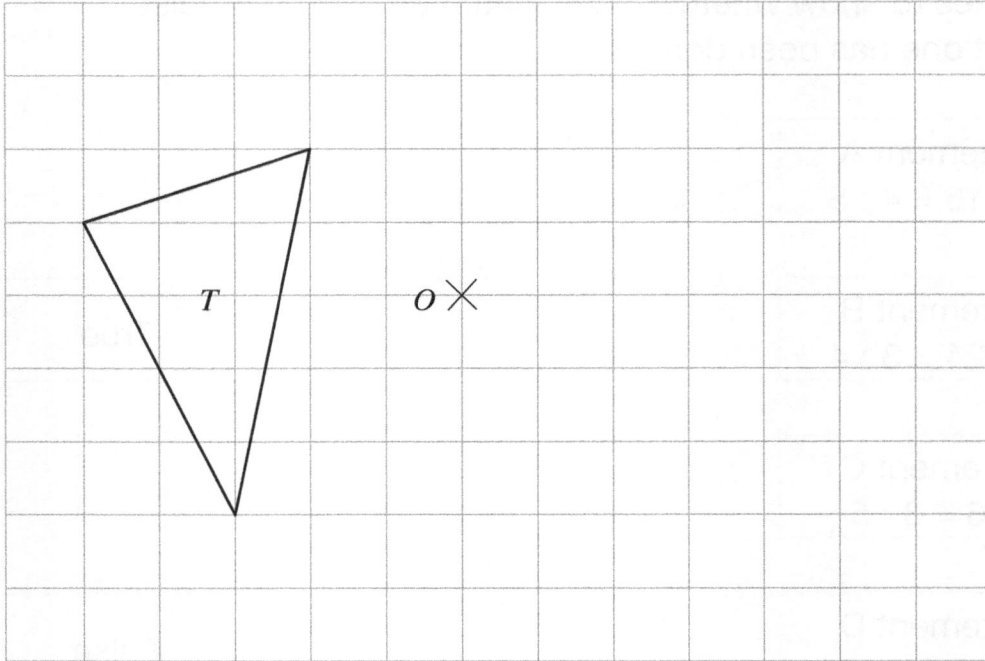

[1]

(b) Rotate quadrilateral Q about the centre O by 90°, clockwise.

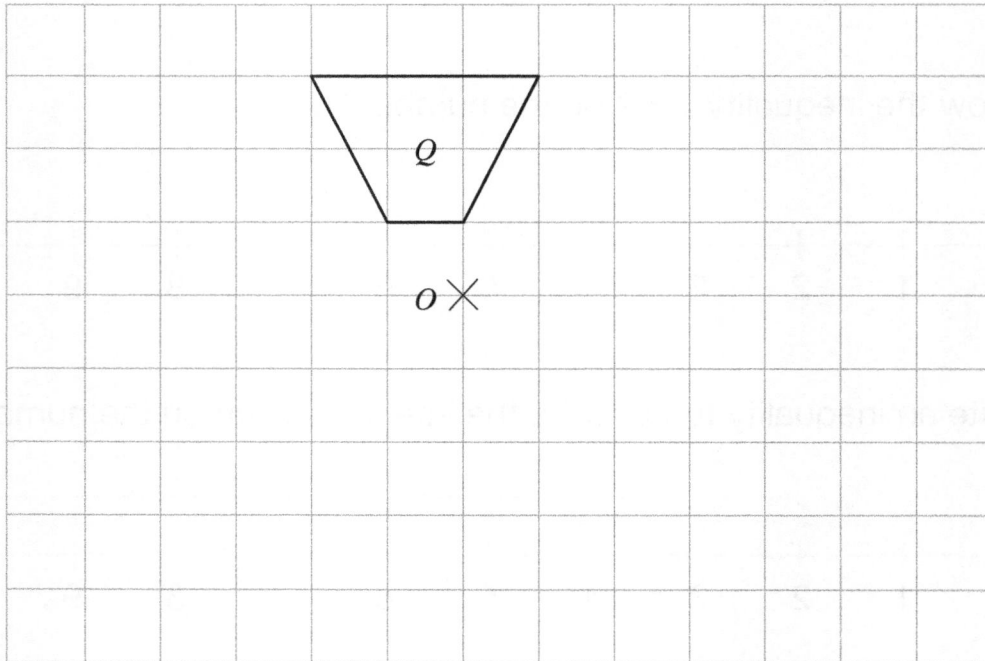

[1]

9 The table shows the sizes of 90 apples.

Size	Number of apples
Small	25
Medium	35
Large	30

Draw a pie chart to represent this information.

[3]

10 Tia and Maryam share 45 postage stamps in the ratio 2 : 7

Calculate the number of stamps that Maryam receives.

_____

[2]

11 The diagram shows two rhombuses drawn on a grid.

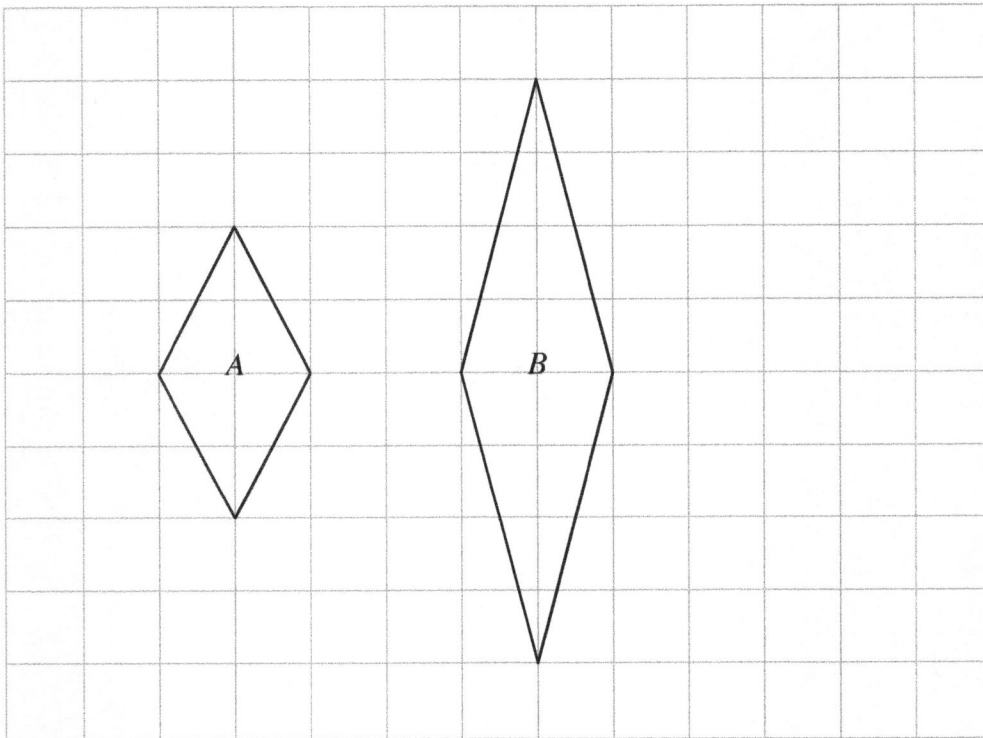

Chetan says that Rhombus B is an enlargement of Rhombus A.

Tick (✓) to show if Chetan is correct or not.

Chetan is correct ☐   Chetan is not correct ☐

Give a reason for your answer.

_____

_____

[1]

12 Here is a recipe to make biscuits.

> **Recipe**
> 70 g sugar
> 200 g flour
> 130 g butter
> 2 eggs
> 40 g dried fruit
>
> *Makes 20 biscuits*

Amir has 320 g of flour.
He has lots of the other ingredients.

Find how many of these biscuits Amir can make.

[2]

Part 2: Calculators allowed

You may use a calculator for this part of the Assessment Task.

13 Draw a ring around the ratio that is equivalent to 1 : 4

       2 : 5   0.5 : 2   4 : 14   0.4 : 1

                                                                                         [1]

14 A school sells 120 tickets for a concert.

Tickets are either for a child or for an adult.
The waffle diagram shows the number of each type of ticket it sells.

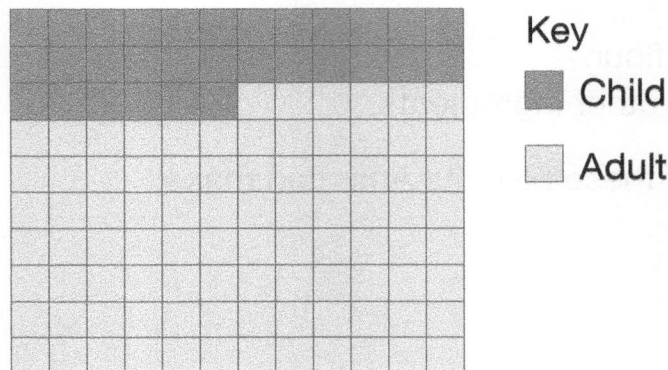

Key
- ■ Child
- □ Adult

Draw a ring around the percentage of child tickets sold.

       25%   30%   75%   90%

                                                                                         [1]

15 Draw a ring around the number that completes this statement.

                 12 out of 25 = _____%

      12   30   40   48

                                                                                        [1]

16 A rectangle R is shown on the grid.

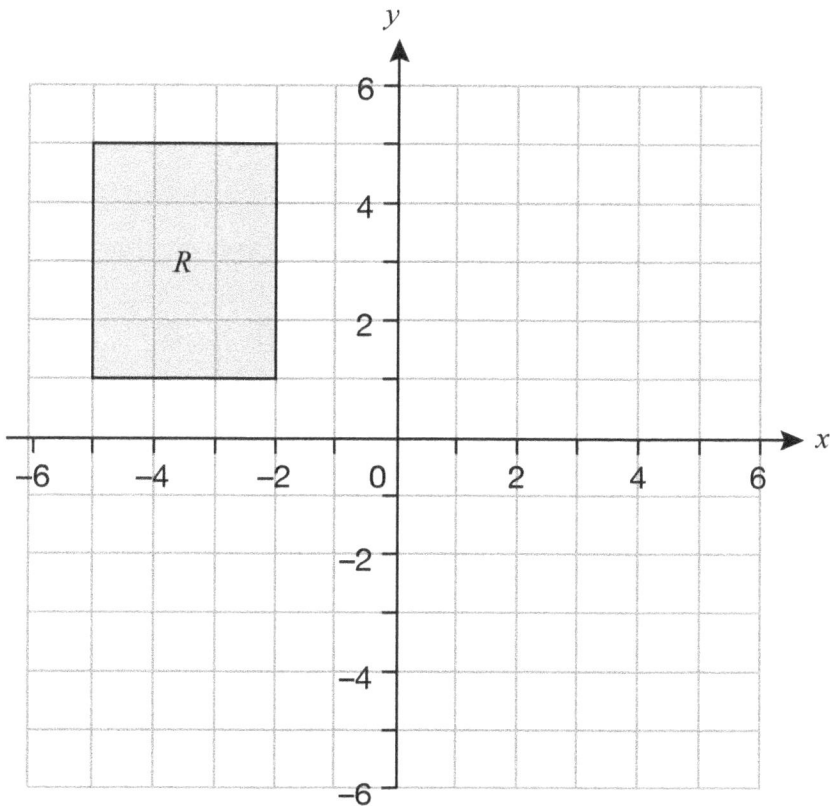

Reflect rectangle R in the y-axis.

[1]

17 (a) Find 400% of $75

$_____

[1]

(b) Find 0.4% of 4500

_____

[1]

18 An interval is defined by the inequality $x < 9$

Draw a ring around all the values in the list below that are included in this interval.

11   8.3   0   9   12.5

[1]

19 The table shows the wheel diameter and the mass of five bicycles.

Diameter (cm)	65	70	68	60	72
Mass (kg)	14.8	19.4	17.6	16.2	17.8

Draw a scatter graph to show this information.

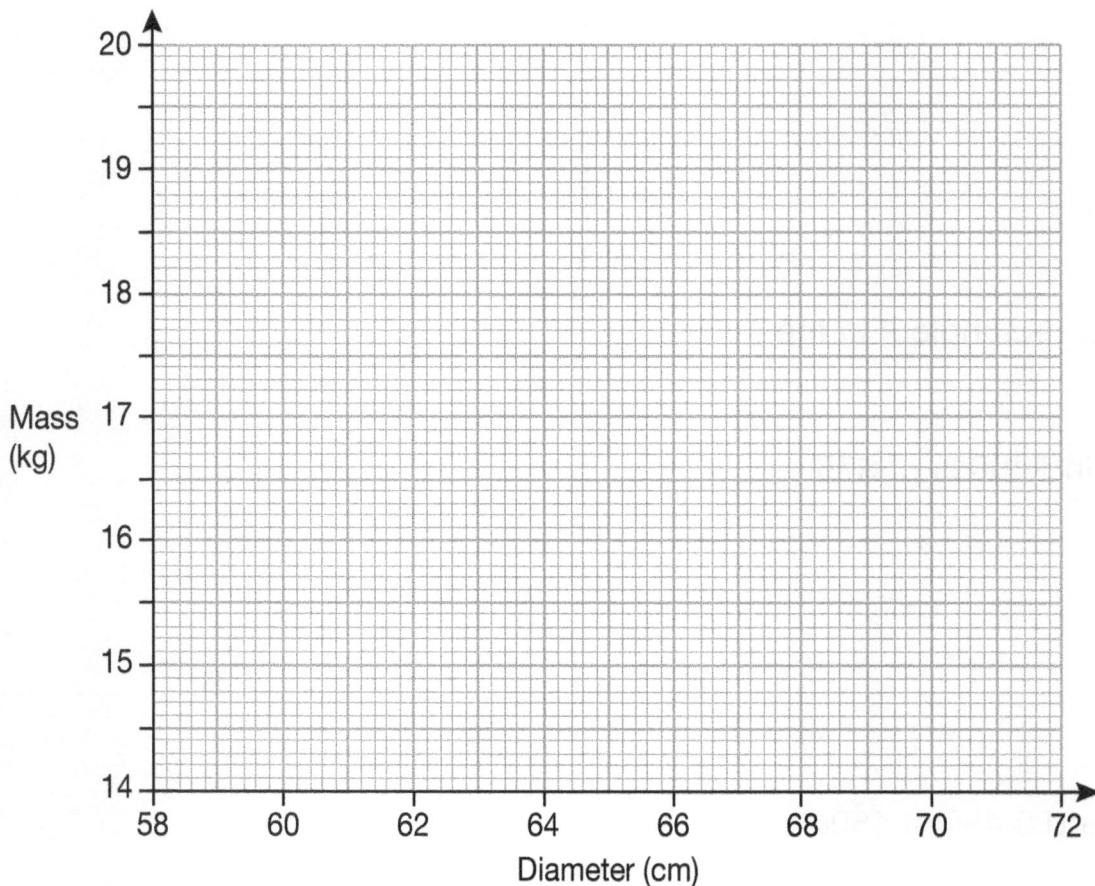

[2]

20 Write a number in each gap to make correct statements.

The distance between (3, 4) and (3, 9) is _____ units.

The distance between (6, 7) and (_____, 7) is 2 units.

The distance between (1, _____) and (4, 5) is 3 units.

[2]

21 Zoya thinks of a number, n.

She multiplies it by 6 and then she adds 4
Her answer is 52

By forming and solving an equation in n, find the number Zoya first thought of.

$n =$ _____

[2]

22 A triangle T is shown on the grid.

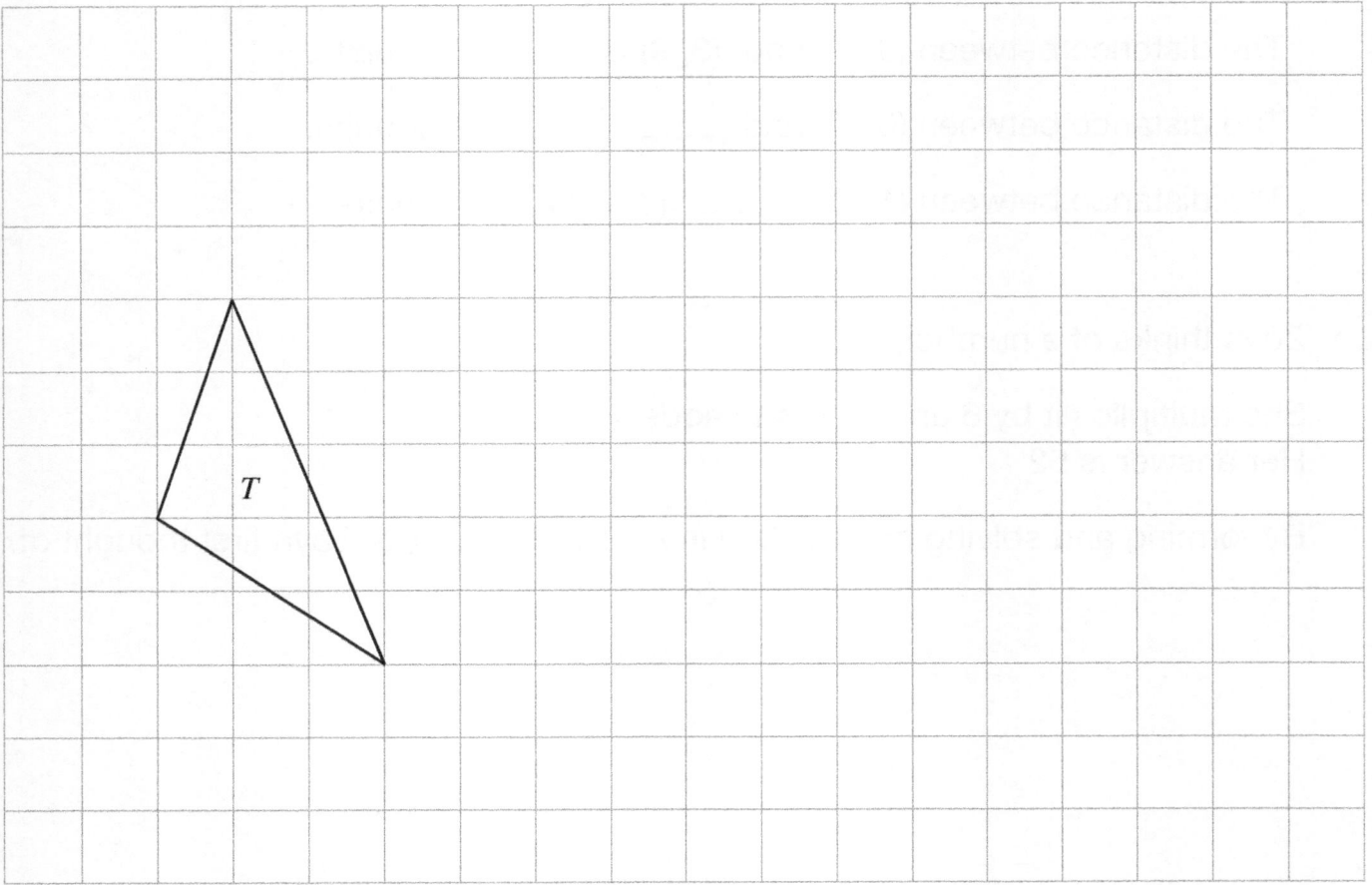

Enlarge triangle T by scale factor 2

[2]

23 Solve the equation $35 - 4y = 7$

$y =$ _____

[2]

24 A shop sells lemons and oranges.

Sophia buys 3 lemons for $0.96

Jagesh buys 7 oranges for $2.59

Yelda has $10
She buys 8 lemons.

Show that Yelda can buy at most 20 oranges with the money she has remaining.

[3]

Total marks: $\frac{}{40}$

Enter the marks for each question in the unshaded cells below.

Question	Transformations	Percentages	Presenting and interpreting data 2	Equations and inequalities	Ratio and proportion
1					
2					
3					
4					
5					
6					
7					
8					
9					
10					
11					
12					
13					
14					
15					
16					
17					
18					
19					
20					
21					
22					
23					
24					
Total	/9	/5	/8	/8	/10

Some of the questions test your skills at Thinking and Working Mathematically.
Write your marks for these questions in the grid below.

Question number	6	11	18	20	24	Total
Thinking and working mathematically						/9

The areas of the test that I am pleased with are

_____

_____

_____

The areas of the test that I found harder are

_____

_____

_____

Set yourself TWO targets.

TARGET 1

_____

_____

TARGET 2

_____

_____

Assessment Task 6

Answer **all** questions.
Total marks for this Assessment Task: 40
You will need mathematical instruments.

> Topics tested:
> Chapter 23: Probability 2
> Chapter 24: Sequences
> Chapter 25: Accurate drawing
> Chapter 26: Thinking statistically
> Chapter 27: Relationships and graphs

Part 1: Calculators not allowed

Do not use a calculator for this part of the Assessment Task.

1 A line has equation $y = x + 5$
Draw a ring around the coordinates of a point that lies on the line.

      (0, 0)   (1, 5)   (2, 10)   (3, 8)   [1]

2 Maddie has a spinner.
She spins it 40 times.
The spinner lands on the blue section on 10 of the spins.

Draw a ring around the relative frequency of the spinner landing on the blue section.

      0.1   0.14   0.25   0.4   [1]

3 The table shows how the students in two classes travelled to school on one day.

	Walk	Car	Bus
Class A	17	5	8
Class B	19	2	10

Draw a ring around the most appropriate diagram for showing the information in the table.

      Scatter diagram   Dual bar chart

      Line graph   Venn diagram   [1]

4 The nth term of a sequence is given by the formula $n + 9$

(a) Find the 4th term in the sequence.

_____

[1]

(b) Which term in the sequence is equal to 16?

_____

[1]

5 (a) Draw a line parallel to the line AB that passes through point C.

$C \times$

A ————————————————— B

[1]

(b) Draw a line perpendicular to the line PQ that passes through point R.

P

R
$\times$

Q

[1]

6 **(a)** y is equal to 20 more than x.

Write this rule as a linear function.

$y = \underline{\hspace{4cm}}$

[1]

(b) 1 dollar = 80 rupees.

d = number of dollars and r = number of rupees.

Write a rule connecting r and d.

$\underline{\hspace{5cm}}$

[1]

7 Sienna wants to find the average colour of front doors for the houses on her street.

She says, "I will use the median."

Tick (✓) to show if the median is a suitable average for Sienna to use.

Median is appropriate ☐   Median is not appropriate ☐

Give a reason for your answer.

_____

_____

[1]

8   Karl draws this waffle diagram to show the types of fruit tree growing in a field.

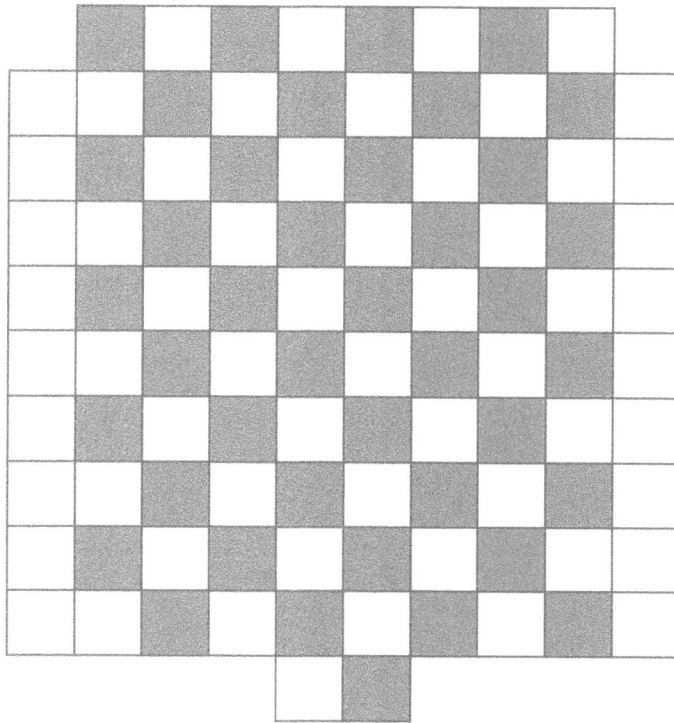

Key

■ plum

□ apple

Draw the waffle diagram in a more appropriate way so that it is easier to compare the number of each type of tree in the field.

Key

■ plum

□ apple

[3]

9 **(a)** Complete the table of values for $y = x + 4$

x	−2	−1	0	1	2	3	4
y			4				

[1]

(b) Draw the graph of $y = x + 4$ for values of x between −2 and 4

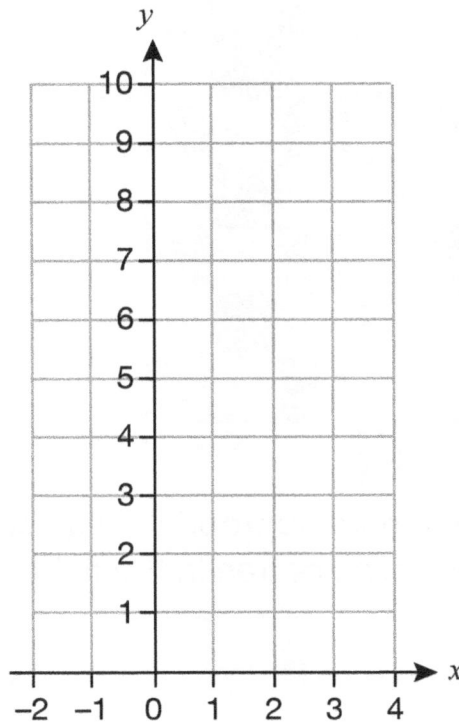

[2]

10 Complete the gaps with two numbers chosen from the box.

A biased dice is thrown _____ times.

The dice lands on 6 on _____ of the throws.

The relative frequency of getting a 6 is $\frac{3}{20}$

```
3
              10
         12
                 25
   80
          100
```

[1]

11 The diagram shows a sketch of a quadrilateral.

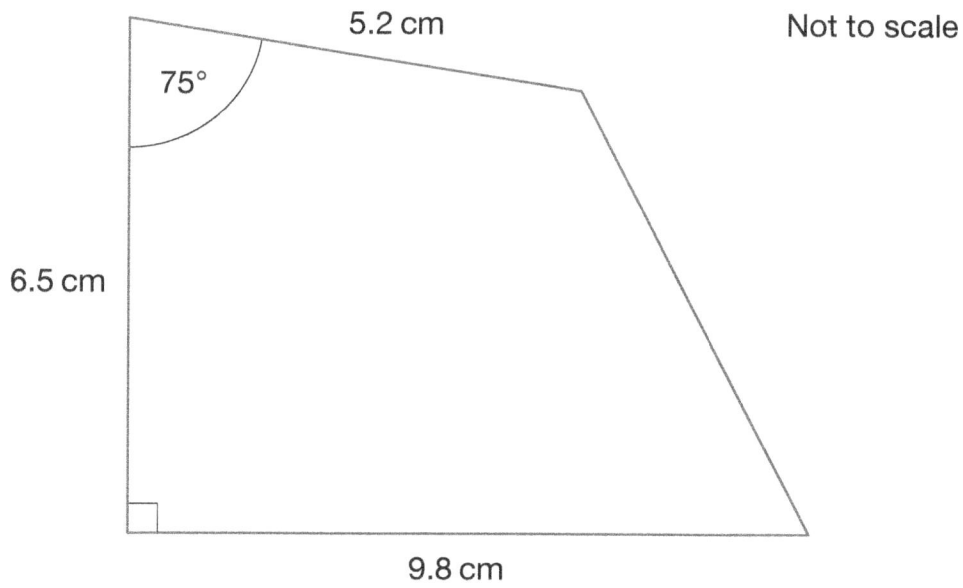

5.2 cm

Not to scale

75°

6.5 cm

9.8 cm

Use a ruler, set square and protractor to draw this quadrilateral accurately.

[3]

Part 2: Calculators allowed

You may use a calculator for this part of the Assessment Task.

12 Here is an object made from 6 cubes.

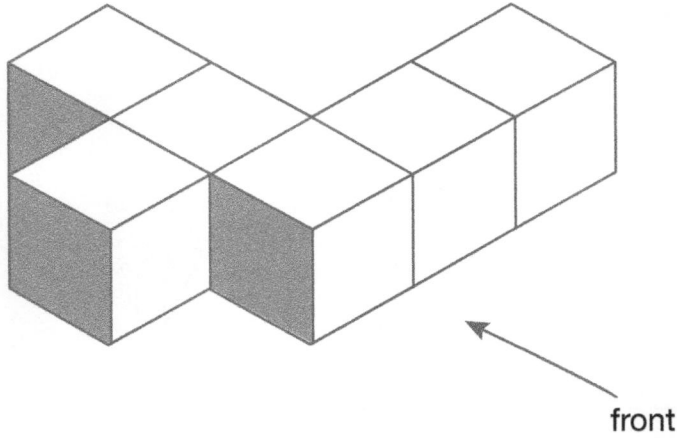

front

Draw a ring around the front elevation of the object.

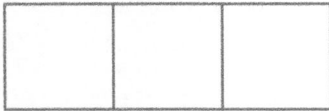

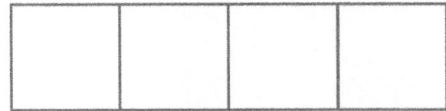

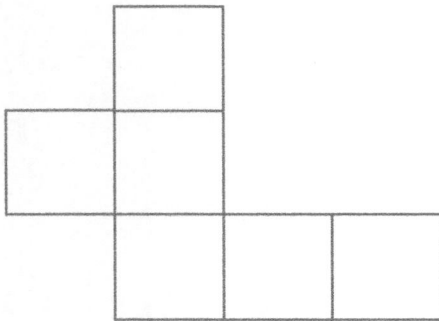

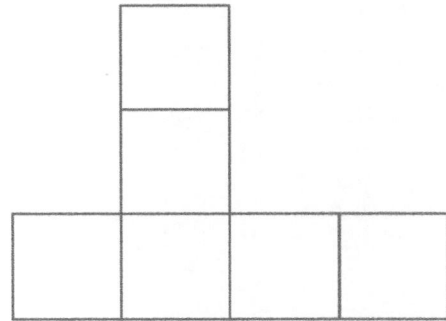

[1]

13 The term-to-term rule of a sequence is 'add 3'

The first term of the sequence is 4

Draw a ring around the 5th term in the sequence.

8   13   16   19

[1]

14 Raj draws a plan of his bedroom using a scale of 1 cm : 0.5 m
On the plan, one of his walls has a length of 8 cm.

Draw a ring around the real length of this wall.

4 m   7.5 m   8 m   16 m   [1]

15 Match the equation of each line to the correct description.

| $x = 5$ |

| $y = 4$ |

| $y = -2$ |

| Parallel to the x-axis |

| Parallel to the y-axis |

[1]

16 Write the missing terms in this linear sequence.

31, 24, _____, 10, _____   [1]

17 Geeta and Karin each conduct an experiment by repeatedly throwing a biased coin.
Here are their results.

	Geeta's results	Karin's results
Heads	17	46
Tails	33	74

(a) Use Geeta's results to estimate the probability that the coin lands on heads.

_____
[1]

(b) Explain why Karin's results would give a better estimate of the probability than Geeta's results.

_____

_____
[1]

18 A school records the number of students absent on each of the last 10 days.

　　　5　　7　　4　　8　　27　　6　　3　　5　　7　　9

(a) Find the mean number of students absent.

_____

[2]

(b) Find the median number of students absent.

_____

[1]

(c) The school wants to use the average that best represents the data.

Tick (✓) the average they should use.

mean ☐　　　　　median ☐

Give a reason for your answer.

_____

_____

[1]

19 The first four terms of a sequence are 7, 8, 9, 10

Write down the nth term rule for the sequence.

_____

[1]

20 A map is drawn to a scale of　1 : 50 000
A lake is 1200 metres in length.

Find the length of the lake on the map.
Give your answer in centimetres.

_____ cm

[2]

21 The travel graph shows Amol's journey from his home to his friend's house.

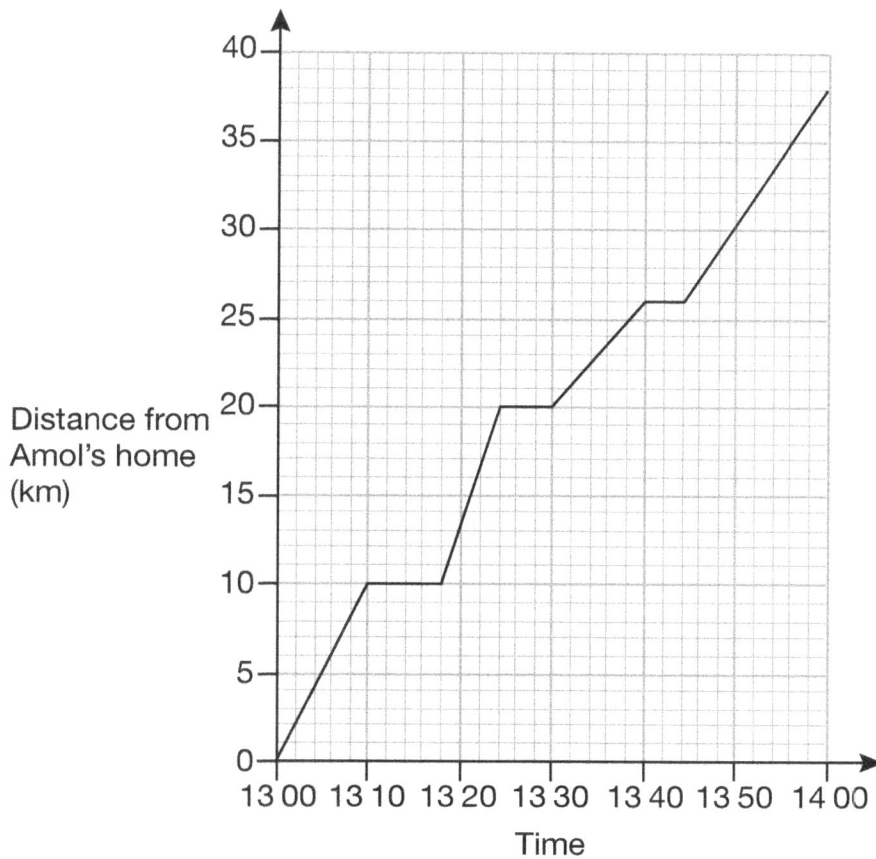

(a) Amol arrives at his friend's house at 14 00

Find the distance from Amol's house to his friend's house.

_____ km

[1]

(b) Amol stopped three times on the journey.

Find the total amount of time that Amol was not moving.

_____ minutes

[1]

22 This graph can be used to convert between US dollars and Saudi riyal.

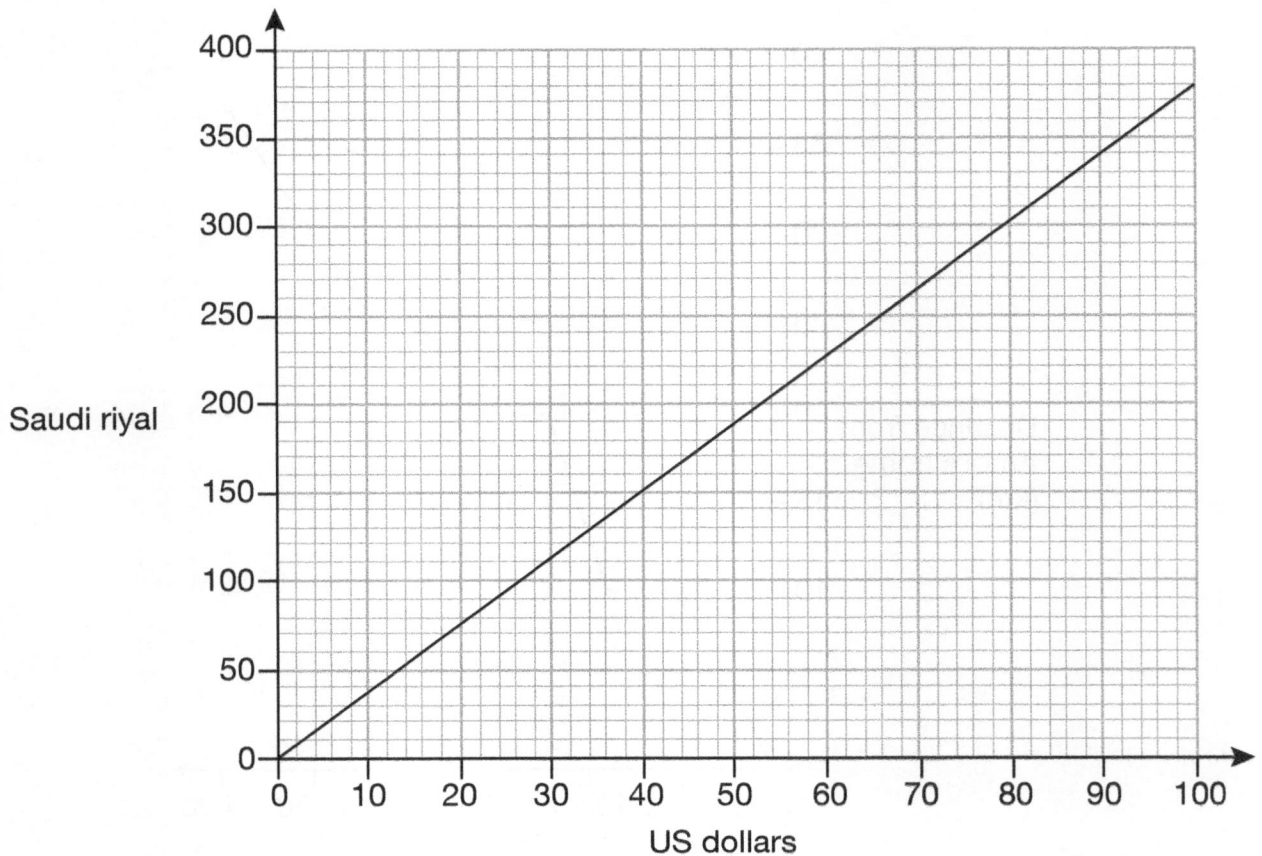

In the United States, a phone costs $800
In Saudi Arabia, the same phone costs 3100 Saudi riyal.

Use this information and the graph to find the difference in the cost of the phone in the two countries.

Give your answer in Saudi riyal.

_____ Saudi riyal

[2]

23 Finn makes a sequence of shapes from square tiles.

The diagram shows the first three shapes in his sequence.

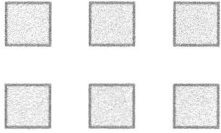 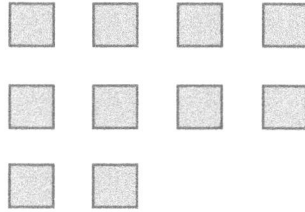 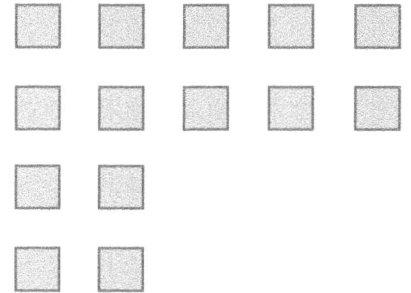

Shape 1　　　　　　**Shape 2**　　　　　　**Shape 3**

Find the number of square tiles needed to make Shape 8.

_____

[2]

Total marks: $\dfrac{}{40}$

Enter the marks for each question in the unshaded cells below.

Question	Probability 2	Sequences	Accurate drawing	Thinking statistically	Relationships and graphs
1					
2					
3					
4					
5					
6					
7					
8					
9					
10					
11					
12					
13					
14					
15					
16					
17					
18					
19					
20					
21					
22					
23					
Total	/4	/7	/9	/9	/11

Some of the questions test your skills at Thinking and Working Mathematically.
Write your marks for these questions in the grid below.

Question number	7	8	10	15	17(b)	18(c)	23	Total
Thinking and working mathematically								/10

The areas of the test that I am pleased with are

_____

_____

_____

The areas of the test that I found harder are

_____

_____

_____

Set yourself TWO targets.

TARGET 1

_____

_____

TARGET 2

_____

_____

End of Book Test: Paper 1

Answer **all** questions.
Total marks for this paper: 50
You will need mathematical instruments for this test.

Calculators not allowed

1 The diagram shows a circle and a line that touches it at one point.

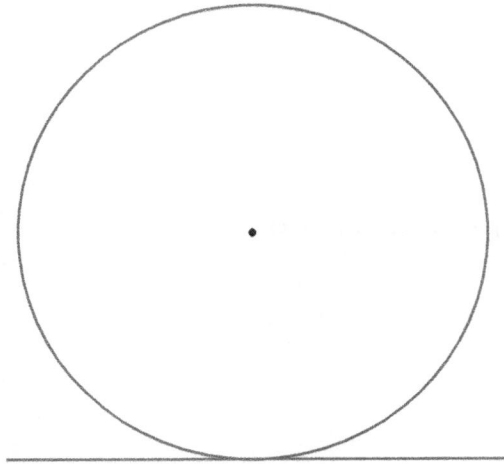

Draw a ring around the name given to this type of line.

      tangent   chord   diameter   radius

[1]

2 Draw a ring around the value of 3×10^4

      120   3000   30 000   810 000

[1]

3 Draw a ring around the expression that is equivalent to $5k - k + 2k$.

      $2k$ $4k$ $6k$ $8k$

[1]

4 A pyramid has a hexagonal base.

Draw a ring around the number of edges that the pyramid has.

          6   7   8   12

[1]

5 Draw a ring around the value of $-2 - (-6)$

          4   8 -8 -4

[1]

6 The pie chart shows the favourite flavours of ice cream for 120 people.

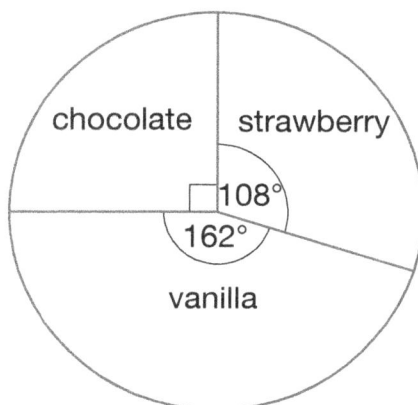

chocolate | strawberry
108°
162°
vanilla

Draw a ring around the number of people who said strawberry was their favourite flavour.

         30   36   54   108

[1]

7 Tick (✓) to show if each statement is true or false.

	True	False
$\sqrt{36} = 6$	☐	☐
$2^3 = 6$	☐	☐
$\sqrt[3]{18} = 6$	☐	☐

[1]

8 **(a)** Here is a function machine.

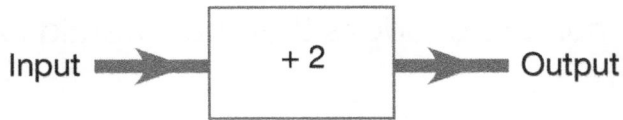

Input ➡ +2 ➡ Output

Complete this mapping diagram for the function machine.

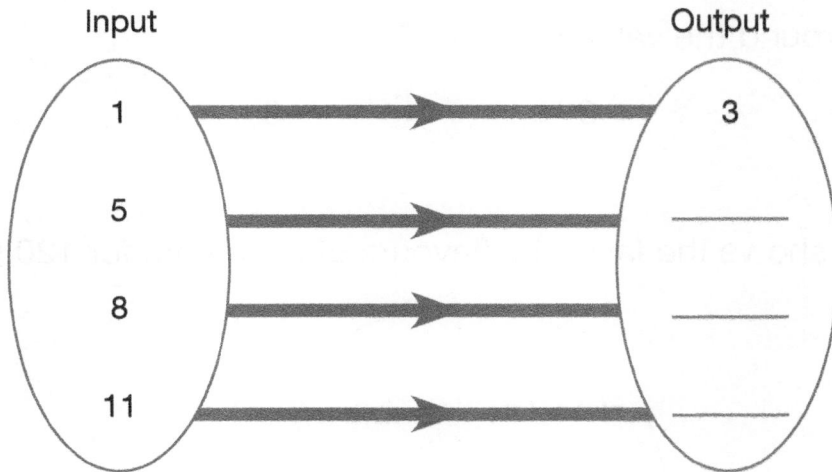

Input

1

5

8

11

Output

3

_____

_____

_____

[2]

(b) Here is an input-output table for a different function machine.

Input	Output
1	5
4	20
7	35

Write the rule in the function machine.

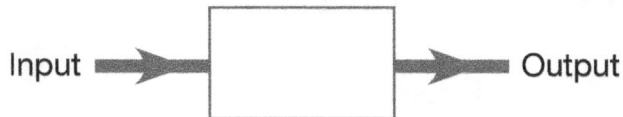

Input ➡ [   ] ➡ Output

[1]

9 Write 0.9 as a fraction and as a percentage.

Fraction _____   Percentage _____%

[1]

10 Here is a triangle T.

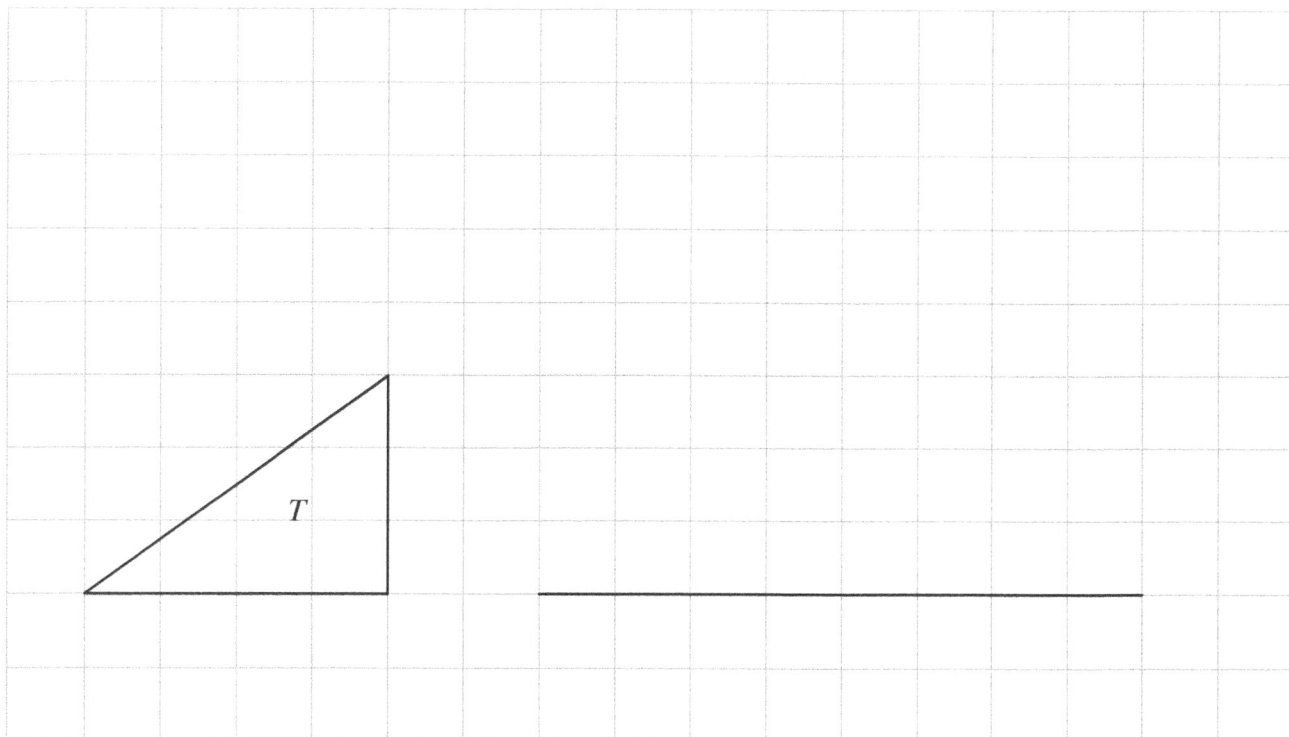

Draw on the grid an enlargement of triangle T, scale factor 2
One side has been drawn for you.

[1]

11 Iqbal counts the number of eggs in 20 bird nests.

Number of eggs	Frequency
4	7
5	5
6	6
7	2

(a) Write down the modal number of eggs in a nest.

_____

[1]

(b) Find the range of the number of eggs.

_____

[1]

12 (a) Find $\frac{1}{4} \times \frac{3}{7}$

_____

[1]

(b) Find $\frac{5}{8} \div \frac{3}{4}$

Simplify your answer.

_____

[2]

13 The diagram shows three angles around a point.

Not to scale

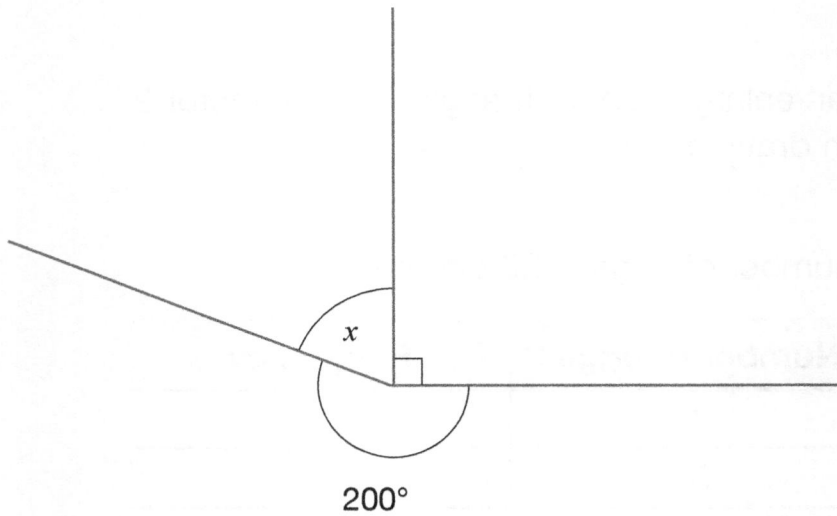

200°

Find the size of the angle x.

$x =$ _____ °

[1]

14 Write each of the numbers below in the Carroll diagram to show if they are divisible by 4 or by 9.

128   774   252   436   546

	Divisible by 4	Not divisible by 4
Divisible by 9		
Not divisible by 9		

[2]

15 (a) Calculate $20 + 12 \div 3$

_____

[1]

(b) Complete the calculation below by writing a whole number or decimal in each gap.

$2.3 \times 11 = 2.3 \times (10 + \underline{\quad\quad}) = 23 + \underline{\quad\quad} = \underline{\quad\quad}$

[2]

16 (a) Write down the equation of a line that is parallel to the y-axis.

_____

[1]

(b) Write down the equation of the line that passes through (2, 4) and is parallel to the x-axis.

_____

[1]

17 The diagram shows a prism made from joining two cuboids.

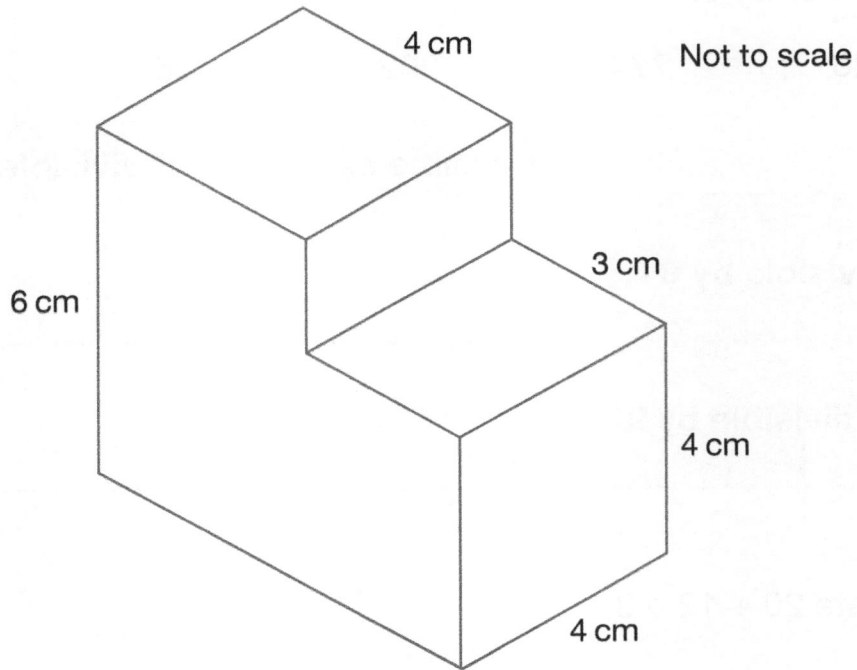

4 cm

Not to scale

3 cm

6 cm

4 cm

4 cm

Calculate the volume of the prism.

_____ cm³

[2]

18 Draw the graph of $y = x - 1$ for values of x between -2 and 3

You may use the table to help you.

x	-2	-1	0	1	2	3
y						

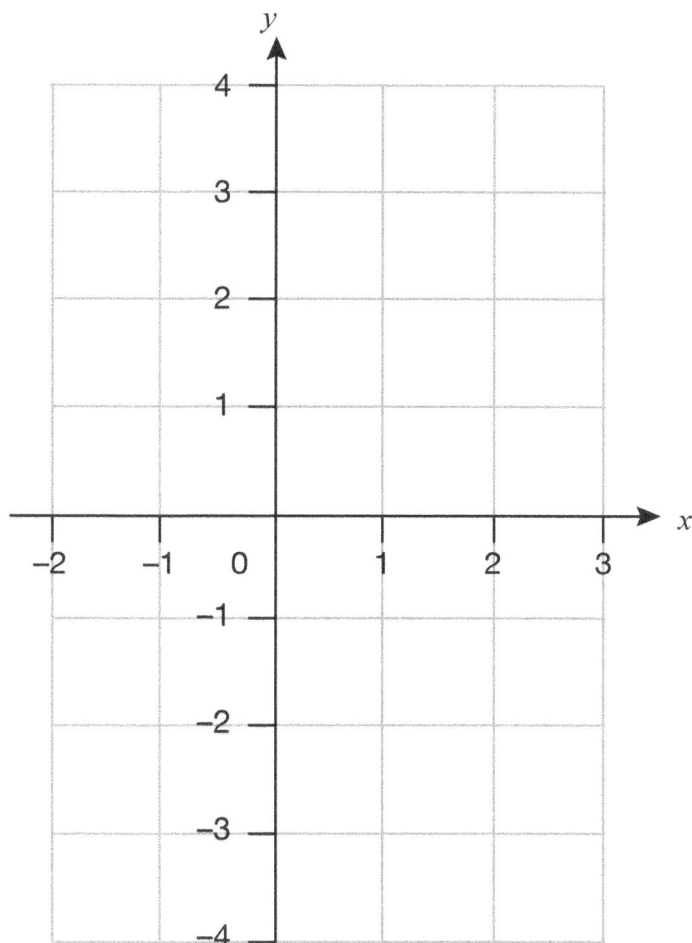

[2]

19 A bag contains 12 cards.

Each card has a regular polygon drawn on it.

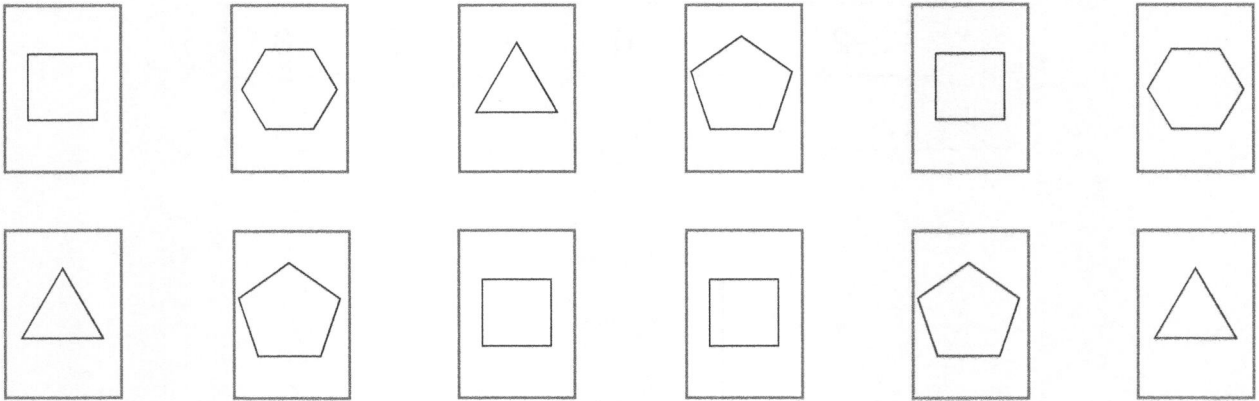

A card is picked at random from the bag.

Find the probability that the card:

(a) contains a triangle

_____

[1]

(b) has a shape with more than 4 sides.

_____

[1]

20 A cake has mass 120 grams.
Antonio cuts the cake into two pieces in the ratio 3 : 5

Find the mass of the smaller piece.

_____ grams

[2]

21 Each statement below is incorrect.

Statement 1: *The lowest common multiple of 8 and 12 is 96*

Statement 2: *The highest common factor of 36 and 48 is 6*

Write each statement to make it correct.

Statement 1: *The lowest common multiple of 8 and 12 is* _____

Statement 2: *The highest common factor of 36 and 48 is* _____

[2]

22 A pentagon P is shown on the grid.

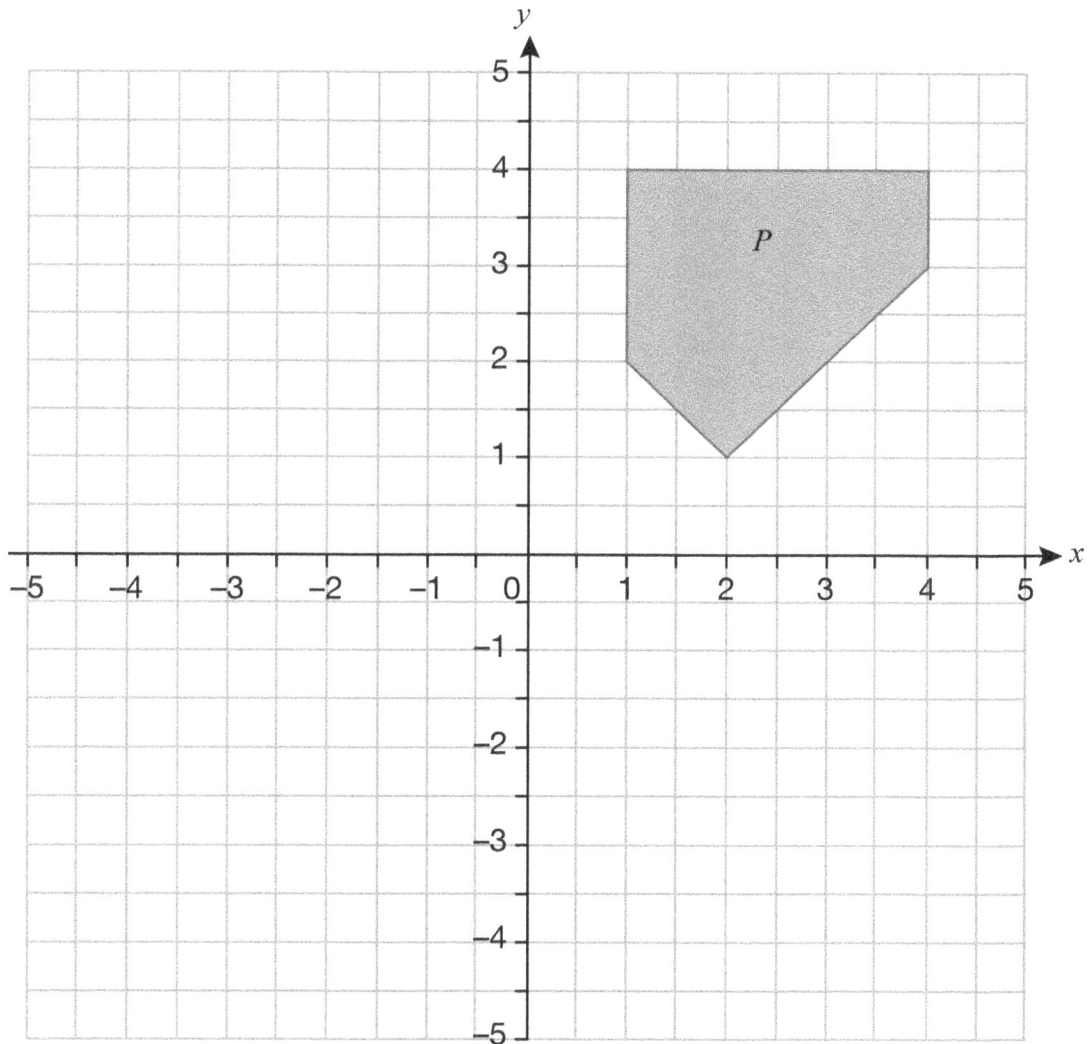

Reflect pentagon P in the y-axis.

[1]

23 Find the value of $3\frac{5}{6} + 1\frac{4}{9}$

Give your answer as a mixed number in its simplest form.

_____

[2]

24 Complete these two statements by writing integers.

(a) $6 \times (-7) =$ _____

[1]

(b) _____ $\div$ _____ $= -8$

[1]

25 The diagram shows a kite.

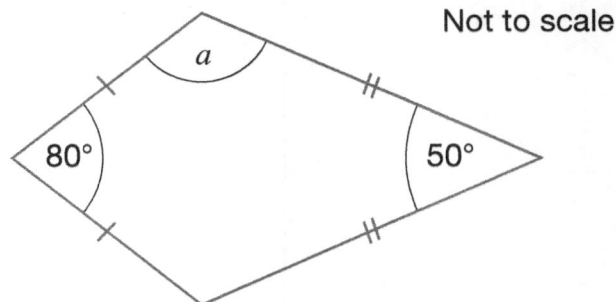

Not to scale

Find the size of angle a.

$a =$ _____ °

[2]

26 $3x + 2 = 38$

Find the value of $2x + 3$

_____

[3]

27 Rhianna asks some adults and some children to vote for their favourite type of fruit.

The table summarises her results.

Type of fruit	Adults	Children
Banana	10	19
Apple	8	6
Mango	22	15

Draw a compound bar chart to represent Rhianna's data.
Remember to complete the key and the axes.

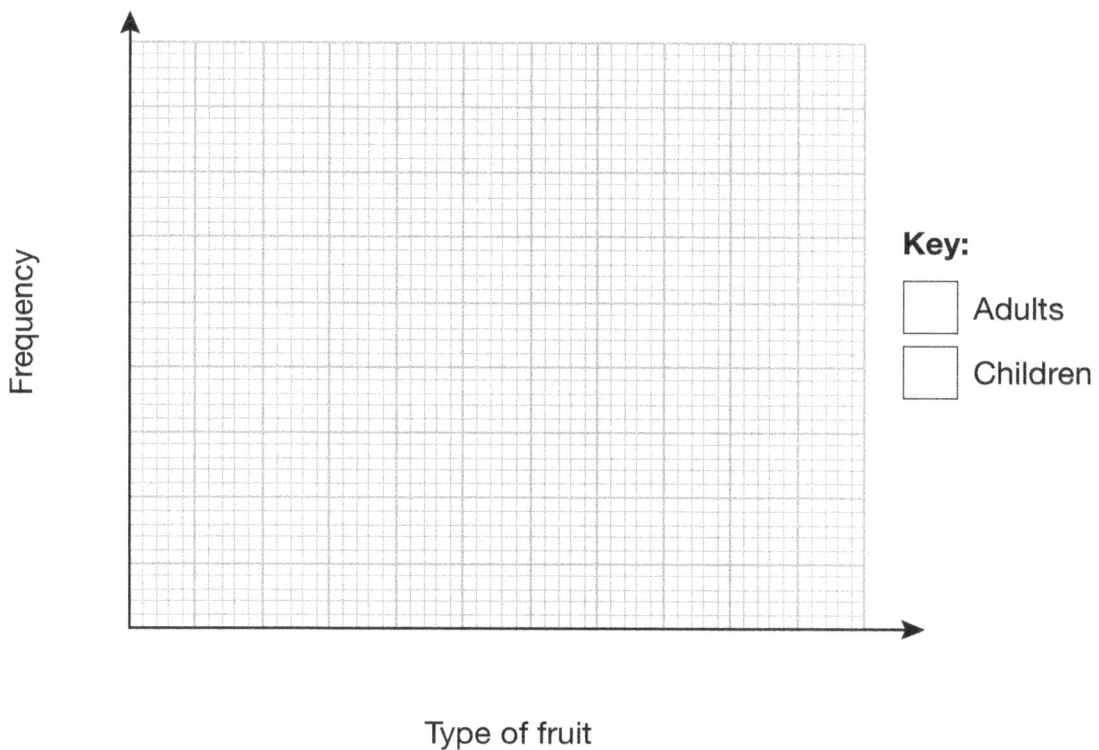

Frequency

Key:

☐ Adults

☐ Children

Type of fruit

[3]

28 Work out 4.6 + 1.65 − 7.942

[2]

Total marks: $\dfrac{}{50}$

End of Book Test: Paper 2

Answer **all** questions.
Total marks for this paper: 50
You will need mathematical instruments for this test.
You may find tracing paper useful.

Calculators allowed

1   If $m = 6$, find the value of $4m$.

   Draw a ring around the answer.

   10   24   46   64

   [1]

2   Draw a ring around the one statement that is true.

   $0.25 < 0.2$ $0.194 > 0.6$ $0.034 < 0.12$ $0.587 > 0.6$

   [1]

3   An ordinary six-sided dice is thrown.

   Draw a ring around the term that describes the chance that the dice will land on a number greater than 1.

   certain   unlikely   even chance   probable

   [1]

4   A square has an area of $1\,cm^2$.

   1 cm

   Not to scale

   Draw a ring around the area of the square in mm^2.

   $10\,mm^2$ $100\,mm^2$ $1000\,mm^2$ $10\,000\,mm^2$

   [1]

5 Draw a ring around the number of lines of symmetry in a regular octagon.

2   4   8   16

[1]

6 Water is poured into a container which is wider at the bottom than at the top.

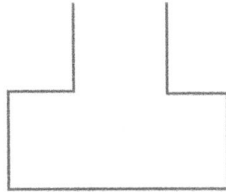

Draw a ring around the graph that shows the height of water in the container plotted against time.

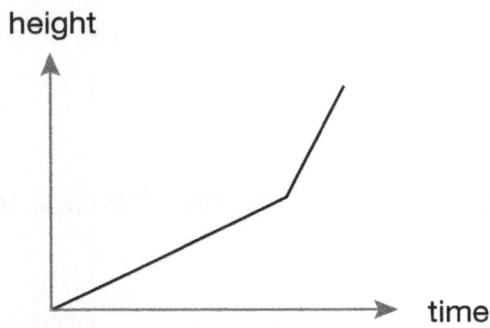

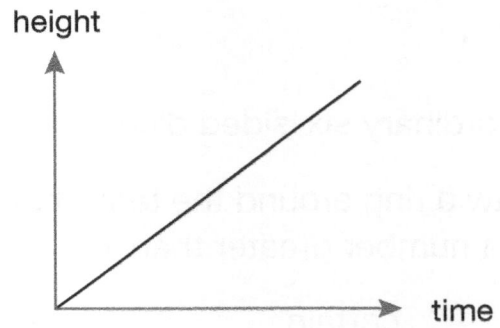

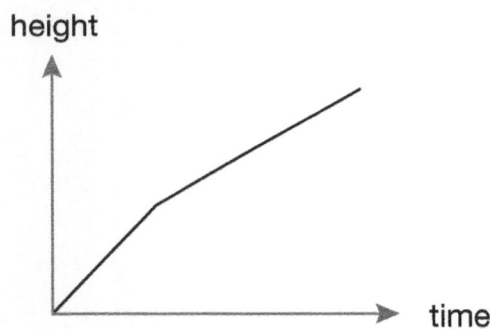

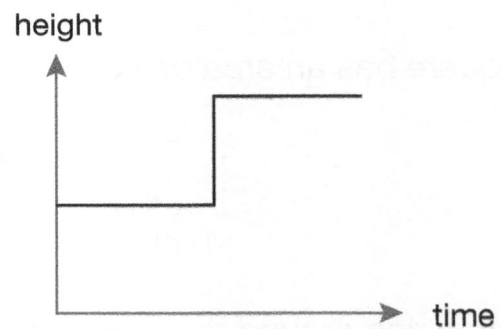

[1]

7 Here is an expression:

$$4t + 7$$

Draw lines to show if each statement is true or false.

| The coefficient of t is 4 |

| True |

| $4t$ is a constant |

| False |

| 7 is a term in the expression |

[1]

8 A lion is n years old.

(a) An elephant is 16 years older than the lion.

Write an expression in terms of n for the age (in years) of the elephant.

_____

[1]

(b) A giraffe is four times as old as the lion.

Write an expression in terms of n for the age (in years) of the giraffe.

_____

[1]

9 Simplify the ratio 25 : 35

_____ : _____

[1]

10 A shop sells loaves of bread.

Key

small

large

The diagram shows the number of small loaves and the number of large loaves it sold one day.

Compare the number of small loaves sold with the number of large loaves sold.

_____

_____

[1]

11 The diagram shows an angle a.

Not to scale

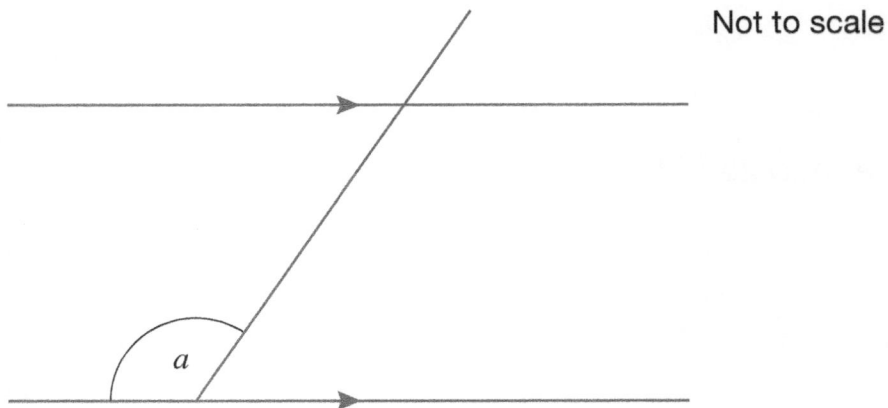

Mark on the diagram two other angles that have the same size as angle a.

[1]

12 Here is a sequence of patterns made from straight lines.

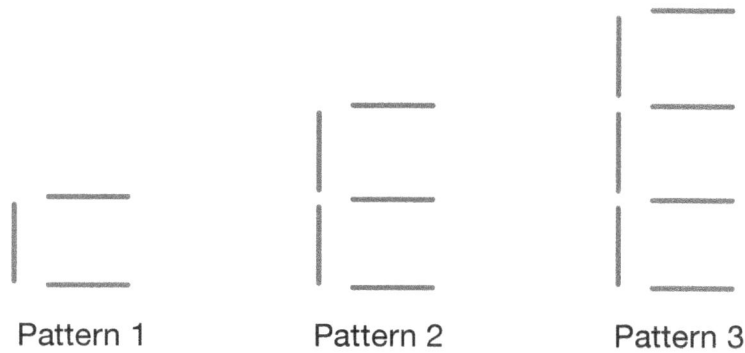

| Pattern 1 | Pattern 2 | Pattern 3 |

(a) Complete the table.

Pattern number	1	2	3
Number of lines	3		

[1]

(b) Find the number of lines needed to make Pattern 5

_____

[1]

13 The diagram shows two congruent triangles.

Not to scale

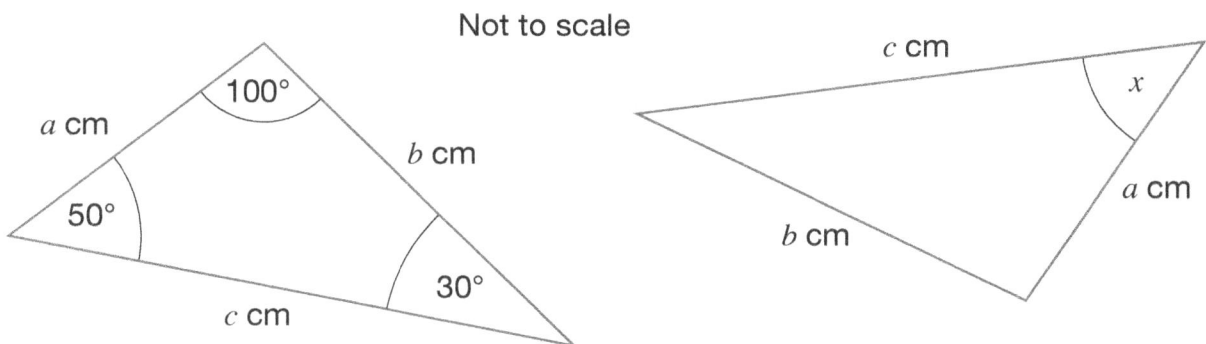

Write down the size of angle x.

$x =$ _____ °

[1]

14 Here is a fair spinner with coloured sections.

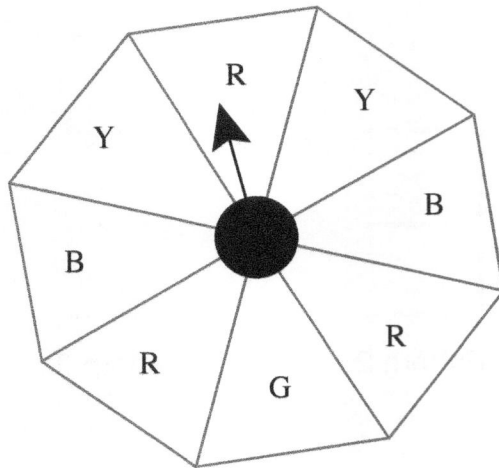

Key
R = red
Y = yellow
G = green
B = blue

The spinner is spun.

Tick (✓) to show if these statements are true or false.

	True	False
The possible outcomes are red, yellow, green and blue	☐	☐
The probability the spinner lands on red is $\frac{1}{4}$	☐	☐

[1]

15 The diagram shows an open interval.

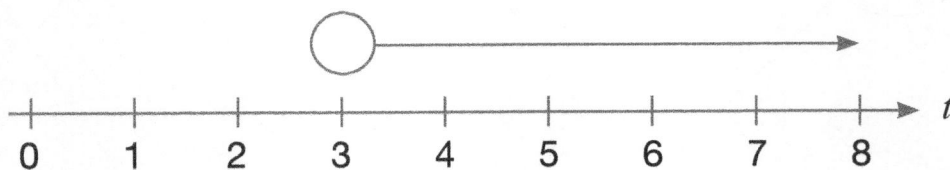

Write this interval as an inequality.

t _____

[1]

16 (a) Complete the descriptions of the symmetrical properties of each shape.

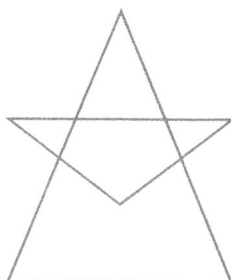

Number of lines of symmetry = _____   Number of lines of symmetry = _____
Rotational symmetry of order _____   Rotational symmetry of order _____

[2]

(b) Here is a square divided into triangles and smaller squares.

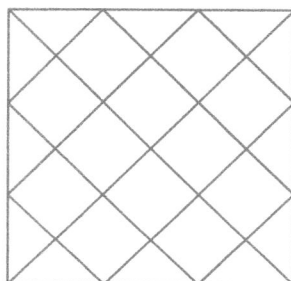

Shade 2 triangles and 4 squares to make a pattern with:
- 2 lines of symmetry **and**
- rotational symmetry of order 2

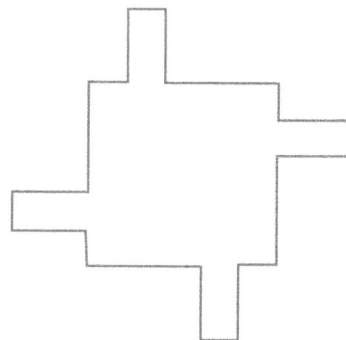

[1]

17 (a) Round 0.284 to 2 decimal places.

_____

[1]

(b) Round 0.47965 to 3 decimal places.

_____

[1]

18 The coordinates of four points are as follows.

$A(4, 2)$ $\qquad$ $B(4, 8)$ $\qquad$ $C(10, 8)$ $\qquad$ $D(4, 10)$

(a) Find the distance between A and D.

_____ units

[1]

(b) Complete each statement using one of the symbols <, > or =

Distance between A and B _____ Distance between B and C

Distance between A and B _____ Distance between B and D

[1]

19 A quadrilateral is shown on the grid.

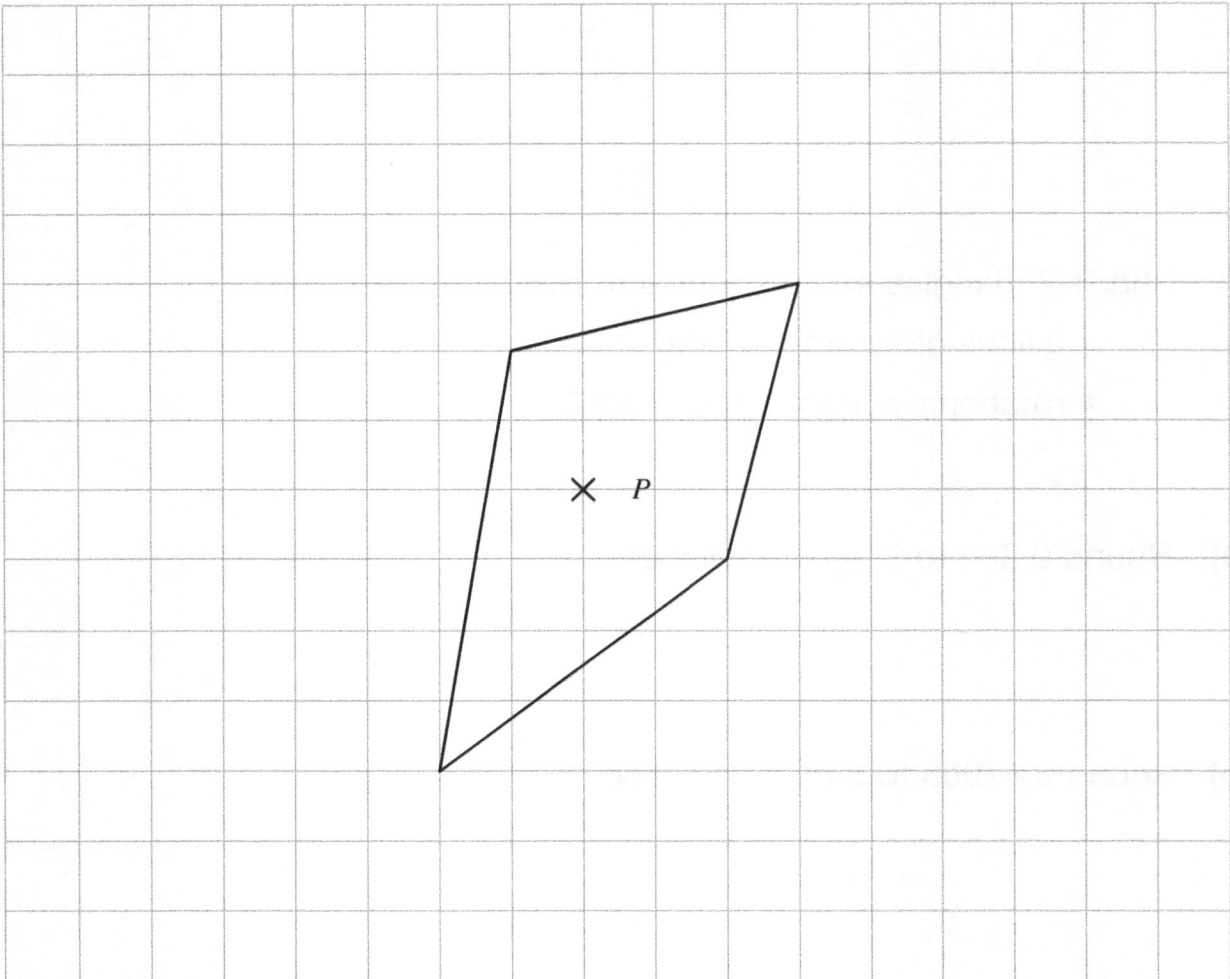

Rotate the quadrilateral by 90° clockwise, centre point P.

[2]

20 Lucy designs a questionnaire to find out the number of times people visited a gym last month.

Here is her question.

> How many times did you visit the gym last month?
> Tick (✓) your answer.
>
> 0–2 ☐   2–4 ☐   4–6 ☐

Write down one problem with her answer options.

_____

_____

[1]

21 (a) Expand $9(4w - 3)$

_____

[1]

(b) Simplify.

$$\frac{11y}{12} - \frac{4y}{12}$$

_____

[1]

22 (a) Find 105% of $480

$ _____

[1]

(b) Anneka has 60 books.

12 of her books are history books.

Find the percentage of her books that are history books.

_____ %

[2]

23 The diagram shows a sketch of a 3D object.

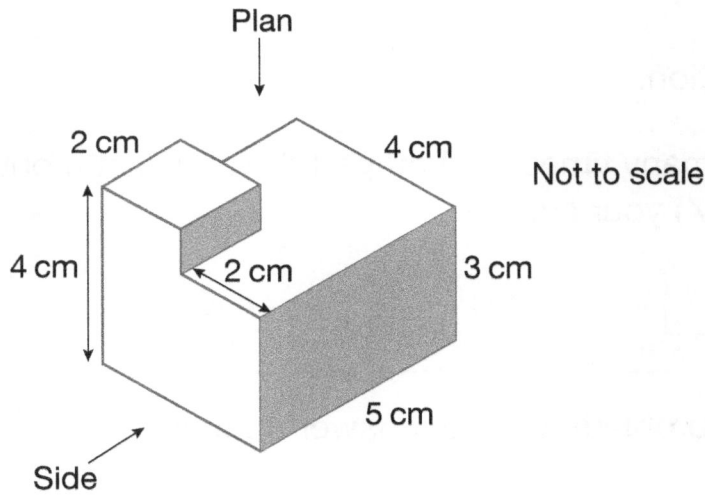

Plan

2 cm   4 cm

Not to scale

4 cm   2 cm   3 cm

Side   5 cm

(a) Tina draws this incorrect plan view of the object on squared paper.

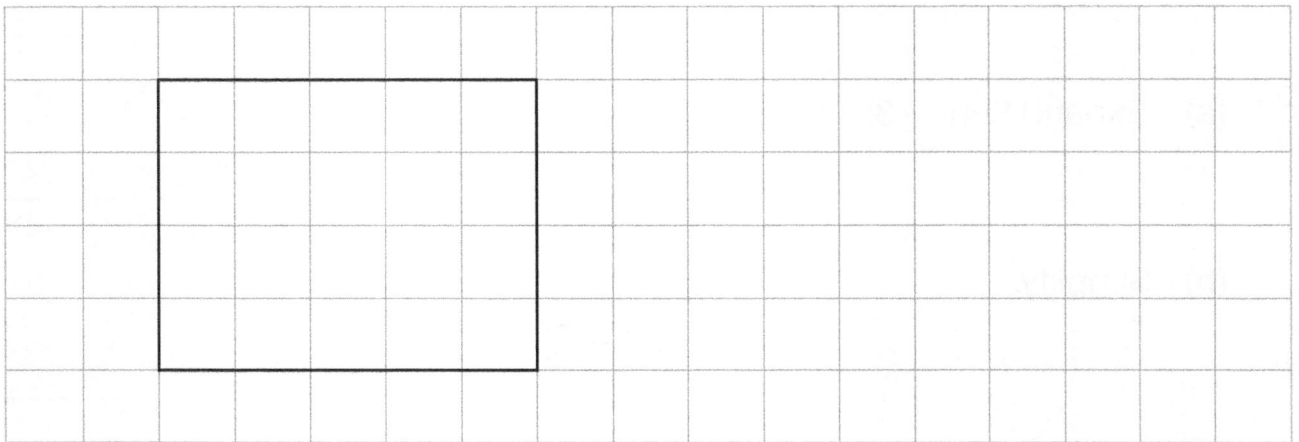

Change Tina's plan view so that it is correct.

[1]

(b) Draw a side elevation of the object from the direction shown on the diagram.

[1]

24 The table shows the ages of some coins.

Age of coin (years)	Frequency
0–5	17
5–10	28
10–15	16
15–20	10
20–25	4

Draw a frequency diagram to show this information.

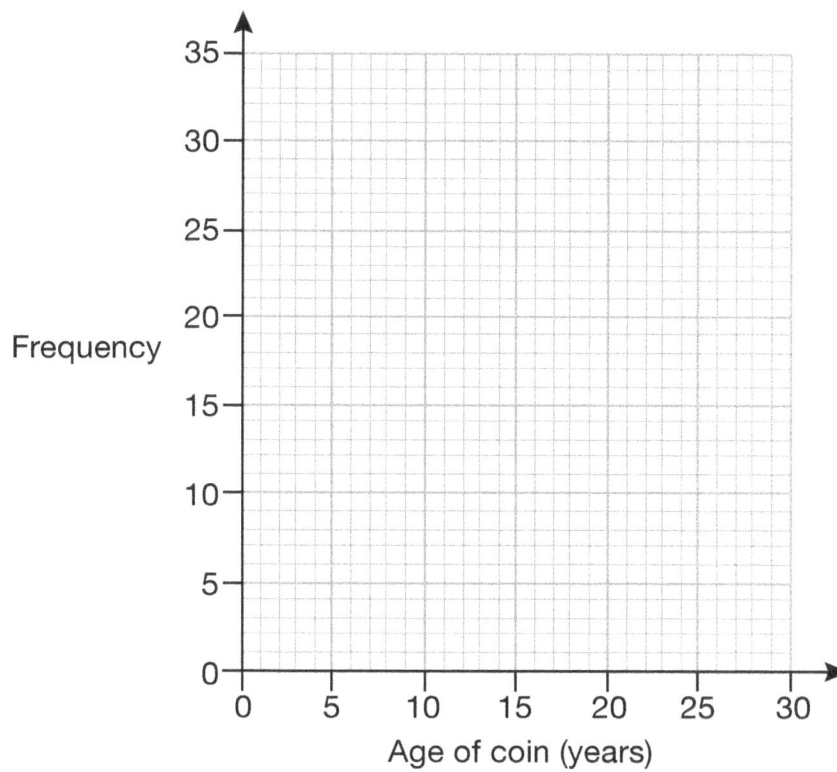

[2]

25 Calculate the area of this shape.

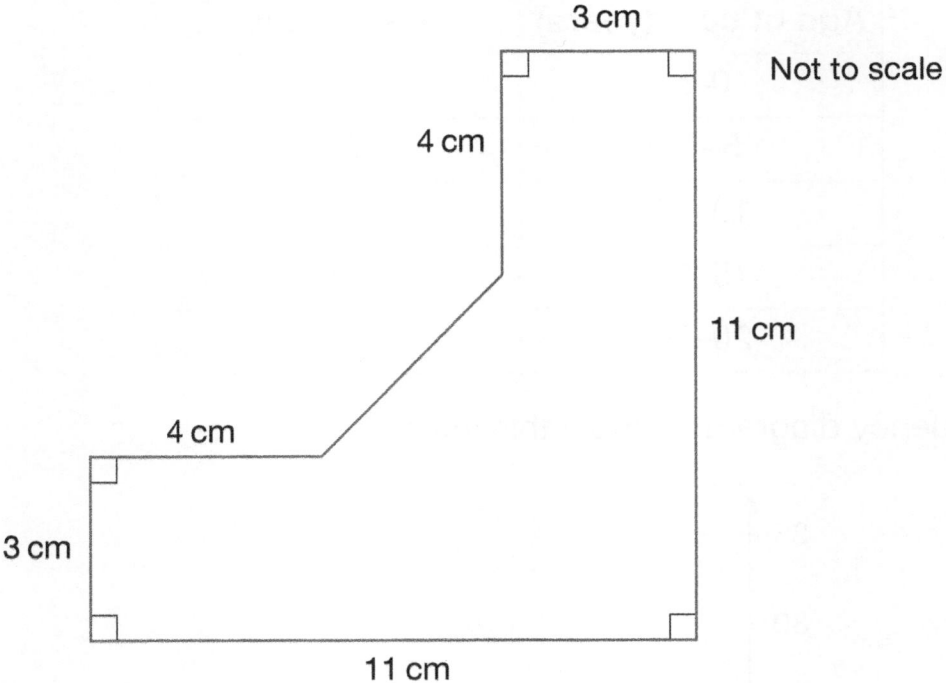

3 cm

Not to scale

4 cm

11 cm

4 cm

3 cm

11 cm

_____ cm²

[2]

26 (a) Krishnan tosses a biased coin repeatedly.

Here are his results.

Outcome	Frequency
Heads	44
Tails	36

Use Krishnan's results to find the relative frequency of his coin landing on a head.

Give your answer as a decimal.

_____

[2]

(b) Georgia throws the same coin **more times** than Krishnan.
She gets the same relative frequency of throwing a head as Krishnan.

Complete the table to show possible results for Georgia.

Outcome	Frequency
Heads	
Tails	

[1]

27 400 South African rand = 3100 Japanese yen.
Kofi buys a television for 27 125 Japanese yen.

Work out the cost of the television in South African rand.

_____ South African rand

[2]

28 Here is a sketch of a trapezium.

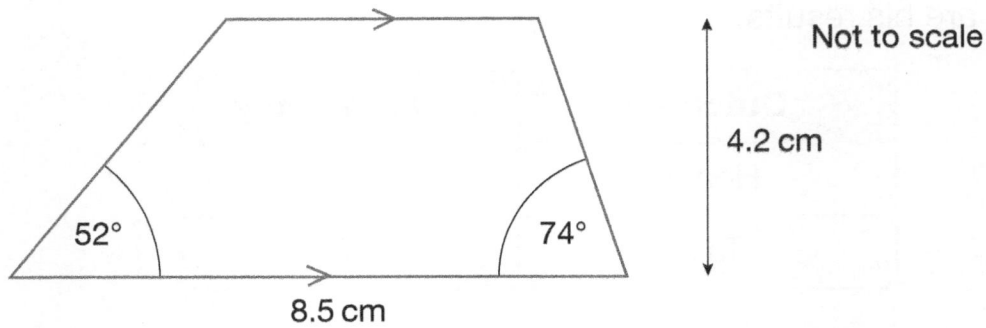

Not to scale

4.2 cm

52°   74°

8.5 cm

Use mathematical instruments to draw the trapezium **accurately**.

[2]

29 The first term of Anton's sequence is 41
The term-to-term rule of his sequence is 'subtract 4'

Suzie has a different sequence.
The nth term of Suzie's sequence is $3n$

Write a number to complete the following statement.

*The 6th term in Anton's sequence is equal to the _____th term in Suzie's
sequence.*

[2]

30 The points (–4, 1), (0, 4) and (1, 12) are all transformed by the same translation.

(–4, 1) is mapped to the point (a, –4)

(0, 4) is mapped to the point (6, b)

(1, 12) is mapped to the point (c, c)

Show that $a + b + c$ is a multiple of 4

[3]

End of Book Test: Self-assessment

Enter the mark for each question for Paper 1 and Paper 2 in the unshaded cells.

Paper 1

Question	Number	Algebra	Geometry and Measure	Statistics and Probability
1				
2				
3				
4				
5				
6				
7				
8				
9				
10				
11				
12				
13				
14				
15				
16				
17				
18				
19				
20				
21				
22				
23				
24				
25				
26				
27				
28				
Total P1	/22	/11	/9	/8

Paper 2

Question	Number	Algebra	Geometry and Measure	Statistics and Probability
1				
2				
3				
4				
5				
6				
7				
8				
9				
10				
11				
12				
13				
14				
15				
16				
17				
18				
19				
20				
21				
22				
23				
24				
25				
26				
27				
28				
29				
30				
Total P2	/9	/12	/20	/9

Overall total Paper 1 + Paper 2:

Total	/31	/23	/29	/17

Total mark: _____ /100

Thinking and working mathematically

Some of the questions test your skills at Thinking and Working Mathematically.
Write your marks for these questions in the grids below.

Paper 1

Question number	7	8(b)	14	16(a)	16(b)	21	24(b)	Total
Thinking and working mathematically								/9

Paper 2

Question number	7	12(b)	14	16(b)	20	23(a)	26(b)	30	Total
Thinking and working mathematically									/10

Overall total: _____ /19

The areas of the test that I am pleased with are

_____

_____

_____

The areas of the test that I found harder are

_____

_____

_____

Set yourself THREE targets.

TARGET 1

_____

_____

TARGET 2

_____

_____

TARGET 3

_____

_____

Mark scheme Task 1

Question	Answer	Mark	Part marks
1	261	1	
2	Chord	1	
3	8	1	
4	All nurses that work in his hospital	1	
5	cylinder	1	
6	The length of a bus	1	
7	−4	1	
8	(12), (24), 36, 48, 60, 72 **and** (15), (30), 45, 60, 75, 90 **and** 60	2	Award 1 mark for (12), (24), 36, 48, 60, 72 **or** (15), (30), 45, 60, 75, 90 **or** 60
9(a)	A correct reason. For example: • Quicker/ easier/ more convenient (than Method 1) • Method 1 would take a long time.	1	Accept equivalents like • Sanjay may not be able to contact all gym members.
9(b)	Ticks 'Not an appropriate sample size' and gives a suitable reason. For example, • 10 is too small a sample size • He should ask more people • The sample may not be representative.	1	Accept equivalents.
10	☑ ☐ ☐ ☑ ☐ ☑	1	All correct.
11	−2 × 14 **or** 14 × −2 **and** 4 × −7 **or** −7 × 4	1	In either order.

Question	Answer	Mark	Part marks
12(a)		1	Line L must touch the circle at A. Allow line L to be just one side of A.
12(b)	Tangent	1	
13		1	All matched correctly.
14	 <u>9</u> edges <u>12</u> edges <u>15</u> edges **and** (The number of edges of a prism must always be a multiple of) 3	2	Award 1 mark for correct number of edges for 2 prisms **or** Award 1 mark for 3
15	−20	2	Award 1 mark for $(\sqrt[3]{125} =)$ 5 **or** for $(5^2) = 25$
16	5016	1	
17(a)	A suitable improvement. For example, • Add a time period • She needs to ask how many times per week/ per month	1	Accept equivalents.
17(b)	There is no option for someone to tick if they don't go to the supermarket **or** If someone goes to the supermarket 4 times, they can tick two boxes	1	Accept equivalents, for example • The intervals don't cover all possible answers • The intervals overlap.

Question	Answer	Mark	Part marks
18	9	2	Award 1 mark for ■ = 36 **or** ◆ = 27
19(a)	24	2	Award 1 mark for an answer of 6, 8 or 12 **or** Award 1 mark for a list of at least 4 factors of both 48 and 72
19(b)	5	1FT	Follow through from (a) if answer was 6, 8 or 12

20	Correct use of the divisibility by 7 rule. For example,
	• 67 – 2 × 2 = 63
	  63 is a multiple of 7 (so 672 is divisible by 7)
	• 67 – 4 = 63
	  63 ÷ 7 = 9 (so 672 is divisible by 7)
		2	Award 1 mark for sight of 63

Mark scheme Task 2

Question	Answer	Mark	Part marks
1	3	1	
2	8	1	
3	200	1	
4	$b - 2$	1	
5	0.5	1	
6	25	1	
7	<table><tr><th>Rounds to 0.51 (to 2 decimal places)</th><th>Rounds to 0.52 (to 2 decimal places)</th></tr><tr><td>0.5137</td><td>0.516</td></tr><tr><td>0.5145</td><td>0.51542</td></tr></table>	2	All numbers correctly placed for 2 marks. Award 1 mark for 3 values correctly placed.
8	18	1	
9	46.4	2	Award 1 mark for answer of 464 or 4.64 or 0.464 **or** Award 1 mark for correct method with 1 arithmetic error.
10(a)	8 written in table	1	
10(b)	25	1	
11	0.0318	1	
12	An expression with value 10 (for example, $2a - b$, $a + b + 2$, $a + 2b$, …) **and** an expression with value 3 (for example, $\frac{a}{b}$, $a - b - 1$, $a + b - 5$, …)	2	For 2 marks, each of the two expressions must contain a term involving a and a term involving b. Award 1 mark for one expression which gives the correct value. For 1 mark, allow expressions involving just one of the variables.
13(a)	1 and 5	2	Award 1 mark for 1 correct answer.

Question	Answer	Mark	Part marks
13(b)	A design with 6 added shaded squares with rotational symmetry order 2 and no lines of symmetry. For example: 	2	Award 1 mark for a design with 2 or 4 added shaded squares with rotational symmetry of order 2 and no lines of symmetry **or** Award 1 mark for a symmetrical design with 6 added shaded squares and rotational symmetry of order 2 **or** Award 1 mark for a design with 6 added shaded squares and no line symmetry with rotational symmetry order 4
14	(Mel multiplies her number by 5 and then subtracts 2) — $5b - 2$ (Kieron multiplies his number by) **4** (and then adds) **9** — $(4c + 9)$	2	Accept equivalent expressions for Mel, for example $b \times 5 - 2$ Award 1 mark for one correct row.
15	 **Key:** ☐ Small ☐ Large	2	For 2 marks, • bars should be separated, have correct height and be a consistent width • division between Small and Large should be at correct position • there should be some way to distinguish Small and Large and key should be completed consistently. Allow bars to be stacked with Small on top of Large. Award 1 mark for one fully correct bar with shading and key **or** Two bars with correct total height and consistent width and positioning (but with problems with wrong or no division or shading).
16	2.371	2	Award 1 mark for an answer starting 2.3 **or** Award 1 mark for rounding their answer with 4 or more decimal places correctly to 3 decimal places.

Question	Answer	Mark	Part marks
17	33	2	Award 1 mark for $xy = 48$ **or** for $3z = 15$
18	Correct demonstration that over half of the students have a hand span of less than 18.5 cm. For example • (Total students =) 100 and (number less than 18.5 =) 55 (which is more than 50) • (number less than 18.5 =) 55 and (number more than 18.5 =) 45	2	Award 1 mark for (Total students =) 100 **or** (number less than 18.5 =) 55 **or** (number more than 18.5 =) 45

Mark scheme Task 3

Question	Answer	Mark	Part marks
1	$2\frac{5}{7}$	1	
2	280°	1	
3	$\frac{2}{21}$	1	
4(a)	5	1	
4(b)	4	1	
5	☐ ✓ ✓ ☐ ☐ ✓	1	All correct.
6	m^3	1	
7	$\frac{8}{5}$ or $1\frac{3}{5}$	2	Award 1 mark for sight of $\frac{24}{15}$ or equivalent unsimplified answer **or** $\frac{2}{3} \times \frac{12}{5}$ **or** for writing with a common denominator, for example $\frac{8}{12} \div \frac{5}{12}$
8	$x = 58(°)$ $y = 122(°)$	2	Award 1 mark for each correct answer **or** Award 1 mark for 180 − 122
9	Correct method for adding $2\frac{5}{6}$ and $1\frac{7}{10}$ leading to the answer $4\frac{8}{15}$ (litres). This should involve correctly converting to common denominators as well as convincing derivation of $4\frac{8}{15}$. For example, • $2 + 1 + \frac{5}{6} + \frac{7}{10} = 3 + \frac{25}{30} + \frac{21}{30}$ and $3 + \frac{46}{30} = 4\frac{16}{30}$ and $4\frac{8}{15}$ • $2 + 1 + \frac{5}{6} + \frac{7}{10} = 3 + \frac{50}{60} + \frac{42}{60}$ and $3 + \frac{92}{60} = 3 + \frac{23}{15}$ and $4\frac{8}{15}$ • $\frac{17}{6} + \frac{17}{10} = \frac{85}{30} + \frac{51}{30}$ and $\frac{136}{30}$ and $\frac{68}{15}$ and $4\frac{8}{15}$	2	Award 1 mark for attempt to convert relevant fractions to a common denominator with at least one numerator converted correctly. For example, • $\frac{5}{6} + \frac{7}{10} = \frac{25}{30} + \frac{21}{30}$ (with at least one of 25 or 21 correct) • $\frac{5}{6} + \frac{7}{10} = \frac{50}{60} + \frac{42}{60}$ (with at least one of 50 or 42 correct) • $\frac{17}{6} + \frac{17}{10} = \frac{85}{30} + \frac{51}{30}$ (with at least one of 85 or 51 correct).

Question	Answer	Mark	Part marks
10	$\frac{7n}{9}$	2	Award 1 mark for a correct but unsimplified answer, for example $\frac{21n}{27}$ **or** Award 1 mark for correct conversion to a common denominator, for example, $\frac{3n}{9} + \frac{4n}{9}$ or $\frac{9n}{27} + \frac{12n}{27}$
11	$12h$	1	
12	2	1	
13	$2k + 6$	1	
14	2	2	Award 1 mark for arranging at least the smallest eight values in increasing order 0 0 0 1 1 1 2 2 (2 3 3 4 4 5 6) **or** Award 1 mark for arranging at least the largest 8 values in decreasing order 6 5 4 4 3 3 2 2 (2 1 1 1 0 0 0)
15	$(u =)$ 61(°)	1	
16(a)	1.6	2	Award 1 mark for sight of 80 **or** Award 1 mark for at least 4 out of these products seen 0 × 9 or 0 1 × 18 or 18 2 × 12 or 24 3 × 6 or 18 4 × 5 or 20
16(b)	✓ ☐ ☐ ✓ ☐ ✓ ✓ ☐	2	Award 1 mark for 3 correct ticks.
17	$(a =)$ 120(°) **and** $(b =)$ 120(°)	1	Both correct.
18	$12x$ $9 - 2a$	2	1 mark for each.
19	$(x =)$ 245(°)	2	Award 1 mark for sight of 115 **or** 360 − 95 − 95 − 55 **or** 95 + 95 + 55

Mark scheme Task 4

Question	Answer	Mark	Part marks
1	30	1	
2	32	1	
3	1.2	1	
4	(see table below)	2	All correct for 2 marks. Accept equivalent fractions in the fraction column. Accept trailing zeros in the decimals, for example 0.30 Award 1 mark for any one fully correct row or column.
5(a)	4	1	
5(b)	22	1	
6	Any value (strictly) between 10 000 and 20 000, for example • 15 000 • 10 001	1	
7	11 **and** 8	2	Award 1 mark for one correct.
8(a)	Any correct demonstration that $\frac{5}{6} > \frac{37}{48}$ For example, • Converting to a common denominator, for example $\frac{5}{6} = \frac{40}{48}$ (which is more than $\frac{37}{48}$) • $\frac{5}{6}$ of 48 = 40 (which is more than 37) • Uses division to attempt decimal equivalents of each fraction, $\frac{5}{6} = 0.8(3\ldots)$ and $\frac{37}{48} = 0.7(7\ldots)$	1	
8(b)	(The smallest fraction is) $\frac{1}{3}$ (The largest fraction is) $\frac{11}{24}$	1	

Question 4 table:

Fraction	Decimal	Percentage
$\frac{3}{4}$	0.75	75%
$\frac{3}{10}$	0.3	30%
$\frac{9}{100}$	0.09	9%

Question	Answer	Mark	Part marks
9	Any vowel on one card and any consonant written on the other card. For example, A and D.	1	
10	Correct demonstration that the area of the shape is 64 (cm²) or that $x = 64$ This should involve sight of both 9×4 or 36 **and** $0.5 \times 7 \times 8$ or 28	3	Allow alternative ways of splitting the shape. Award 1 mark for (area of rectangle =) 9×4 **or** 36 **and** Award 1 mark for (area of triangle =) $0.5 \times 7 \times 8$ **or** 28
11	$7 + (4^2 + 5) \times 2 = 49$	1	Only one set of brackets should be included.
12(a)	103.5%	1	
12(b)	$\dfrac{207}{200}$	2	Award 1 mark for $1\dfrac{7}{200}$ **or** for $\dfrac{their\ 103.5}{100}$ **or** for $1 + \dfrac{3.5}{100}$ **or** for $1 + \dfrac{7}{20} \div 10$
13	$\dfrac{1}{6}$	1	
14	21 cm²	1	
15	$h = 24d$	1	
16	$\dfrac{1}{6}$ $\quad$ (≠) $\quad$ 0.2 $\dfrac{11}{20}$ $\quad$ = $\quad$ 0.55 $\dfrac{7}{8}$ $\quad$ = $\quad$ 0.875 $\dfrac{5}{16}$ $\quad$ ≠ $\quad$ 0.315	2	Award 1 mark for 2 correct symbols.
17	COOKBOOK — C, O, K, B — ☐ ☑ REAPPEAR — R, E, A, P — ☑ ☐ WELLNESS — W, E, L, N, S — ☐ ☑	2	Allow outcomes written in any order. Award 1 mark for one correct row **or** for possible outcomes column filled in correctly **or** for both ticks correct.

Question	Answer	Mark	Part marks
18	✓ ☐ ✓ ☐ ☐ ✓	1	All boxes correct.
19(a)	Any decimal number in the interval $1.49 < x < 1.5$, for example • 1.491 • 1.495 • 1.49999	1	
19(b)	Any mixed number in the interval $2\frac{1}{10} < y < 2\frac{1}{5}$, for example • $2\frac{1}{7}$ • $2\frac{11}{100}$ • $2\frac{2}{15}$	1	
20	5 cm² 700 mm² 0.04 m²	1	
21	280 (cm²)	3	Award 2 marks for (2 ×) 5 × 6 or 30 or 60 **and** (2 ×) 5 × 10 or 50 or 100 **and** (2 ×) 6 × 10 or 60 or 120 **or** Award 1 mark for (2 ×) 5 × 6 or 30 or 60 **or** (2 ×) 5 × 10 or 50 or 100 **or** (2 ×) 6 × 10 or 60 or 120
22	70	2	Award 1 mark for ($x =$) 14 **or** for correctly finding *their* $x \times 5$
23	$b = 60n$	1	Or equivalent, for example $b = 60 \times n$
24	($x =$) 7.5	3	Award 1 mark for (Volume of A =) 7 × 9 × 6 or 378 **and** Award 1 mark for $\dfrac{6 + \textit{their volume of A}}{8 \times 6.4}$

Mark scheme Task 5

Question	Answer	Mark	Part marks
1	(7, 6)	1	
2	$x = 4$	1	
3	125%	1	
4	18	2	Award 1 mark for sight of 27 or 9
5	4	1	
6	Statement A $12 : 15 = 4 : 5$ — True Statement B $18 : 24 = 3 : 4$ — True Statement C $4 : 6 = 3 : 5$ — False Statement D $1.5 : 3 = 1 : 2$ — True Statement E $0.6 : 0.4 = 2 : 3$ — False	2	Award 1 mark for 2 or 3 correct matches.
7(a)		1	Mark intention.
7(b)	$x > 4$ or equivalent	1	
8(a)		1	
8(b)		1	

Question	Answer	Mark	Part marks
9	A pie chart with angles the correct size and with sectors labelled (Small, Medium and Large). For example 	3	Allow ± 2° Angles do not need to be marked on the pie chart. Award 2 marks for a pie chart with all sectors the correct angles but with labels missing **or** a pie chart with 3 labelled sectors and one sector the correct size **or** Award 1 mark for sight of any correct angle (implied by a sector of the correct size).
10	35	2	Award 1 mark for 45 ÷ (2 + 7) or 5 (1 mark can be implied by sight of 10).
11	Ticks Chetan is not correct **and** gives a correct reason. For example • The angles in the two quadrilaterals are different • Rhombus B is not similar to Rhombus A.	1	
12	32	2	Award 1 mark for 200 ÷ 20 or 10 (grams per biscuit) **or** (1 gram of flour makes) 20 ÷ 200 or 0.1 (biscuit) **or** (120 grams makes) 12 biscuits.
13	0.5 : 2	1	
14	25%	1	
15	48	1	

Question	Answer	Mark	Part marks
16		1	
17(a)	($)300	1	
17(b)	18	1	
18	8.3 **and** 0	1	
19	Correct scatter graph. 	2	Allow 0.5 small square tolerance. Award 1 mark for 3 or 4 points plotted correctly.
20	5 4 or 8 5	2	Award 1 mark for correctly completing 1 or 2 of the statements.
21	($n =$) 8 with sight of a correct equation, for example $6n + 4 = 52$	2	Allow $6n = 52 - 4$ or $6n = 48$ as the equation. Award 1 mark for ($n =$) 8 without sight of a correct equation **or** Award 1 mark for sight of a correct equation.

Question	Answer	Mark	Part marks
22	For example 	2	Enlargement can be drawn anywhere on the grid. Award 1 mark for enlarging any one side of the triangle correctly.
23	$(y =)$ 7	2	Award 1 mark for a correct first step. For example, • $35 = 4y + 7$ • $4y = 35 - 7$ or $4y = 28$ • $-4y = 7 - 35$ or $-4y = -28$
24	Correct demonstration that Yelda can buy at most 20 oranges. For example, • (8 lemons cost) ($)2.56 **and** $(10 - 2.56) \div 0.37 = 20.1\ldots$ • 8 lemons and 20 oranges cost ($)9.96 so the cost of 8 lemons and 21 oranges is more than ($)10	3	Award 2 marks for sight of ($)2.56 or ($)7.44 or ($)9.96 or ($)10.33 **or** Award 1 mark for sight of ($)0.32 or ($)0.37

Mark scheme Task 6

Question	Answer	Mark	Part marks
1	(3, 8)	1	
2	0.25	1	
3	Dual bar chart	1	
4(a)	13	1	
4(b)	7(th)	1	
5(a)		1	Line should pass through the cross (1 mm tolerance). Line should be at least half the length of AB.
5(b)		1	Line should pass through the cross (1 mm tolerance). Line may not extend as far as PQ.
6(a)	$(y =) 20 + x$	1	Or equivalent.
6(b)	$r = 80d$ or $r = 80 \times d$	1	Or equivalent.
7	Ticks Median is not appropriate **and** gives a suitable reason. For example <ul><li>Colours can't be ordered</li><li>(You can't find the median as) you can't find the middle colour</li><li>The mode is the only average you can find for colours.</li></ul>	1	

Question	Answer	Mark	Part marks
8	A 10 by 10 square with the plum and apple sections grouped together with shading to match the key. For example. **Key** ☐ plum ☐ apple	3	Award 2 marks for a waffle diagram with 2 of these elements ● 10 by 10 square ● 41 squares shaded ● Shaded squares all grouped together. **or** Award 1 mark for either a 10 by 10 square or for all shaded squares grouped.
9(a)	<table><tr><td>*x*</td><td>−2</td><td>−1</td><td>0</td><td>1</td><td>2</td><td>3</td><td>4</td></tr><tr><td>*y*</td><td>2</td><td>3</td><td>(4)</td><td>5</td><td>6</td><td>7</td><td>8</td></tr></table>	1	All values correct.
9(b)		2FT	FT from *their* (a) if the points are plotted and joined to make a straight line. All 7 points should be able to be plotted on the given grid. Award 1 mark for a correct line but not covering the entire interval from −2 to 4 **or** at least 5 points from *their* table plotted correctly.
10	80 **and** 12	1	

Question	Answer	Mark	Part marks
11	An accurately drawn quadrilateral 5.2 cm Not full size 75° 6.5 cm 9.8 cm	3	1 mm tolerance on the 9.8 cm, 6.5 cm and 5.2 cm sides. 2° tolerance on the 90° and 75° angles. Award 2 marks if at least 2 sides and at least 1 angle are drawn accurately **or** Award 1 mark if at least 2 sides or at least 1 angle are drawn accurately.
12		1	
13	16	1	
14	4 m	1	
15	$x = 5$ $y = 4$ Parallel to the x-axis Parallel to the y-axis $y = -2$	1	
16	17 **and** 3	1	
17(a)	$\frac{17}{50}$ or 0.34	1	Accept equivalent fractions or percentage. Ignore incorrect conversion to a decimal or percentage if a correct fraction is seen.
17(b)	An answer that implies that Karin threw the dice more times.	1	
18(a)	8.1	2	Award 1 mark for sight of 81 **or** for a correct method (attempt to add and divide by 10).
18(b)	6.5	1	

Question	Answer	Mark	Part marks
18(c)	Ticks median **and** gives a suitable reason. For example, The mean is affected by the large value (27) in the data.	1	Allow 'there is an anomalous value in the data'.
19	$n + 6$	1	Or equivalent
20	2.4 (cm)	2	Award 1 mark for 0.024 **or** $1200 \div 50\,000$ **or** $(50\,000\,\text{cm} =)\ 500\ (\text{m})$ **or** $(1200\,\text{m} =)\ 120\,000\ (\text{cm})$
21(a)	38 (km)	1	
21(b)	18 (minutes)	1	
22	An answer between 60 and 140 (Saudi riyal).	2	Award 1 mark for correct strategy for converting $800 into Saudi riyal. For example • reading off at $100 and multiplying by 8 • reading off at $80 and multiplying by 10 **or** Award 1 mark for converting 3100 Saudi riyal into dollars. For example, reading off at 310 riyal and multiplying by 10
23	34	2	Award 1 mark for extending the sequence to at least Shape 5 (6, 10, 14) 18, 22 **or** Award 1 mark for noting the term-to-term rule is Add 4 **or** Award 1 mark for drawing Shape 8

Mark scheme Paper 1

Question	Answer	Mark	Part marks
1	Tangent	1	
2	30 000	1	
3	$6k$	1	
4	12	1	
5	4	1	
6	36	1	
7		1	All correct.
8(a)		2	Award 1 mark for 2 correct values.
8(b)	$\times 5$	1	
9	$\frac{9}{10}$ **and** 90(%)	1	Accept equivalent unsimplified fractions.
10		1	
11(a)	4	1	
11(b)	3	1	
12(a)	$\frac{3}{28}$	1	
12(b)	$\frac{5}{6}$	2	Award 1 mark for $\frac{5}{8} \times \frac{4}{3}$ or equivalent or for $\frac{5}{8} \div \frac{6}{8}$ or equivalent.

Question	Answer	Mark	Part marks
13	70(°)	1	
14	(see table below)	2	Award 1 mark for 3 or 4 numbers entered correctly.

Question 14 table:

	Divisible by 4	Not divisible by 4
Divisible by 9	252	774
Not divisible by 9	128 / 436	546

Question	Answer	Mark	Part marks
15(a)	24	1	
15(b)	1 **and** 2.3 **and** 25.3	2	Award 1 mark for 25.3 **or** for 1 **and** 2.3
16(a)	Any line in the form $x = k$ or equivalent. For example $x = 2$, $x + 1 = 0$	1	$k \neq 0$
16(b)	$y = 4$	1	
17	144 (cm³)	2	Award 1 mark for sight of any of the following • 4 × 4 × 6 or 96 • 4 × 4 × 3 or 48 • 7 × 4 × 6 or 168 • 4 × 3 × 2 or 24 • 4 × 4 × 7 or 112 • 4 × 4 × 2 or 32
18	A ruled graph drawn between (–2, –3) and (3, 2)	2	Award 1 mark for A correctly completed table of values (implied by correctly plotted points) **or** A line with gradient 1 (allow unruled) **or** A line passing through (0, –1) (allow unruled) **or** 6 points from their table of values plotted correctly (must fit on grid).
19(a)	$\frac{3}{12}$ or $\frac{1}{4}$	1	Allow 0.25 or 25%

Question	Answer	Mark	Part marks
19(b)	$\frac{5}{12}$	1	Allow 0.416(6…) or 0.417 or 0.42 or equivalent percentages.
20	45 (grams)	2	Award 1 mark for $\frac{120}{3+5}$ or 15 or 75
21	24 **and** 12	2	Award 1 mark for each answer.
22		1	
23	$5\frac{5}{18}$	2	Award 1 mark for a correct unsimplified mixed fraction/improper fraction **or** correctly converting both $\frac{5}{6}$ and $\frac{4}{9}$ to a common denominator (implied by $\frac{23}{18}$ or equivalent fraction) **or** correctly converting both $\frac{23}{6}$ and $\frac{13}{9}$ to a common denominator.
24(a)	−42	1	
24(b)	Any two integers that complete the calculation correctly. For example, 16 ÷ (−2) or (−8) ÷ 1	1	
25	115(°)	2	Award 1 mark for 360 − 80 − 50 or 230

Question	Answer	Mark	Part marks
26	27	3	Award 2 marks for sight of $x = 12$ **or** Award 1 mark for $3x = 38 - 2$ (= 36) **or** for finding $2x + 3$ for *their x*.
27	A compound bar chart with bars equal width and correct height, axes numbered/ labelled, correct sub-divisions of bars, correct shading and a completed key. 	3	Award 2 marks for any 4 of the following satisfied: ● bars equal width ● vertical axis scale and bars of correct height ● horizontal axis labelled ● correct sub-divisions of bars ● bars shaded with a consistently shaded key. **or** Award 1 mark if any 3 of the bullet points satisfied.
28	−1.692	2	Award 1 mark for sight of 6.25 or (−)3.342 or (−)6.292

Mark scheme Paper 2

Question	Answer	Mark	Part marks
1	24	1	
2	0.034 < 0.12	1	
3	probable	1	
4	100 mm^2	1	
5	8	1	
6		1	
7		1	
8(a)	$n + 16$	1	
8(b)	$4n$	1	
9	5 : 7	1	
10	There were more large loaves sold than small loaves.	1	Or equivalent.
11		1	Both angles marked.

Question	Answer	Mark	Part marks
12(a)	<table><tr><td>**Pattern number**</td><td>1</td><td>2</td><td>3</td></tr><tr><td>**Number of lines**</td><td>3</td><td>5</td><td>7</td></tr></table>	1	
12(b)	11	1	
13	$x = 50°$	1	
14	✓ ☐ ☐ ✓	1	Both boxes ticked correctly.
15	$t > 3$	1	
16(a)	1 0 1 4	2	Award 1 mark for 2 or 3 correct values.
16(b)	2 triangles and 4 squares shaded to make a pattern with 2 lines of symmetry and rotational symmetry order 2	1	For example,
17(a)	0.28	1	
17(b)	0.480	1	
18(a)	8	1	
18(b)	= >	1	Both correct.
19		2	Award 1 mark for a shape of correct size and orientation but incorrect position **or** for 3 correct vertices.

Question	Answer	Mark	Part marks
20	A suitable problem identified. For example • There is no box to tick for someone going to the gym more than 6 times • There are two boxes that can be ticked if you went to the gym 2 times/4 times.	1	Accept • Response boxes do not cover all possible answers • The answer options overlap.
21(a)	$36w - 27$	1	
21(b)	$\frac{7y}{12}$	1	
22(a)	($)504	1	
22(b)	20(%)	2	Award 1 mark for $\frac{12}{60}$ or equivalent **or** $12 \div 60$ (× 100) or 0.2
23(a)		1	
23(b)		1	
24		2	For 2 marks there must not be gaps between the bars. Award 1 mark for 3 or 4 bars correctly drawn with no gaps **or** Award 1 mark for all bars at correct height but with gaps.

Question	Answer	Mark	Part marks
25	65 cm²	2	Award 1 mark for sight of area of a relevant triangle or rectangle: 33 or 24 or 8 or 12
26(a)	0.55	2	Award 1 mark for $\frac{44}{80}$ or equivalent fraction **or** $44 \div 80$ **or** answer of 0.45
26(b)	Any correct table with total frequency > 80 and ratio of heads : tails = 11 : 9 For example, • 88 heads and 72 tails • 55 heads and 45 tails.	1FT	Follow through *their* part (a) – accept tables that give the same relative frequency as found in (a) provided total frequency > 80
27	3500 (South African rand)	2	Award 1 mark for $\frac{27125}{3100}$ or 8.75 or $\frac{3100}{27125}$ or equivalent **or** for $\frac{400}{3100}$ or $\frac{3100}{400}$ or equivalent.
28	An accurate drawing of the trapezium. Not full size 4.2 cm 52° 74° 8.5 cm	2	Tolerance of 2 mm on lengths and 2° on angles. Award 1 mark for at least one accurately drawn length (8.5 cm or 4.2 cm) **and** at least one accurately drawn angle (52° or 74°).
29	7(th)	2	Award 1 mark for sight of 21
30	$a = 2$, $b = -1$ and $c = 7$ **and** $a + b + c = 8$ (which is a multiple of 4)	3	Award 2 marks for sight of 2 of $a = 2$, $b = -1$ and $c = 7$ **or** Award 1 mark for sight of $a = 2$ or $b = -1$ or $c = 7$ **or** Award 1 mark for 6 right, 5 down.